Birds of Prey

American bald eagles, ospreys, hawks, crested caracaras, and burrowing owls

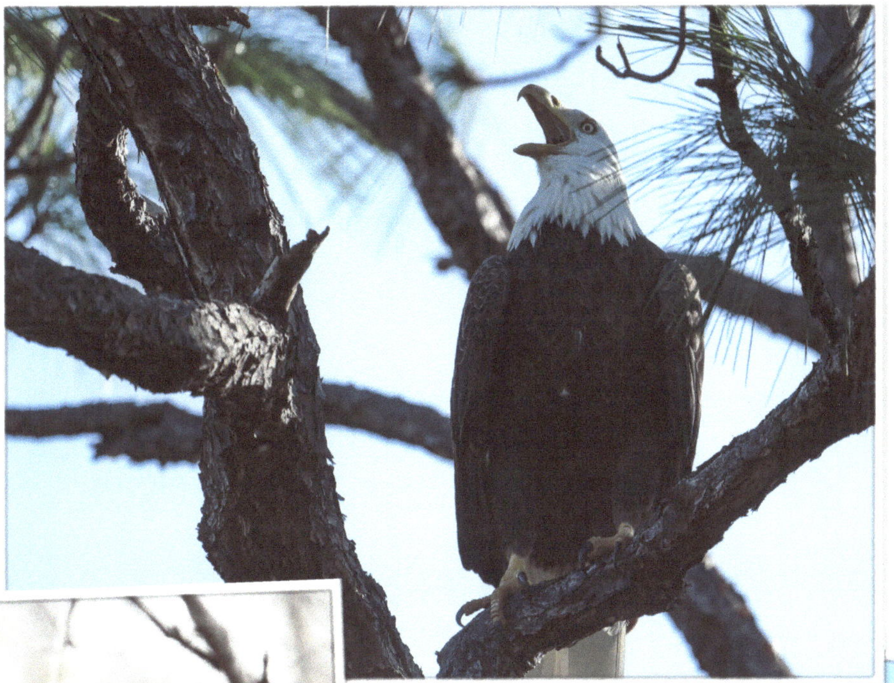

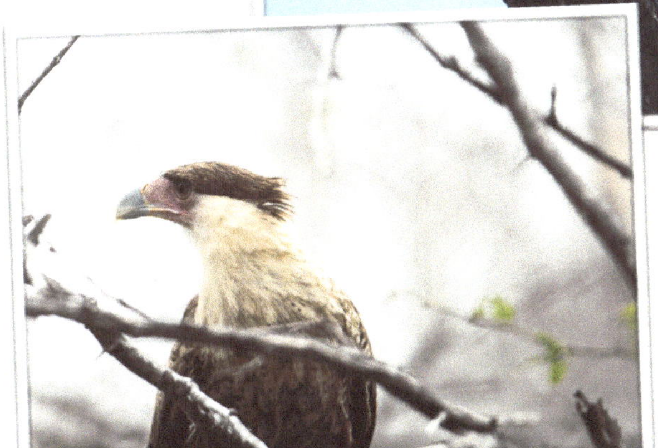

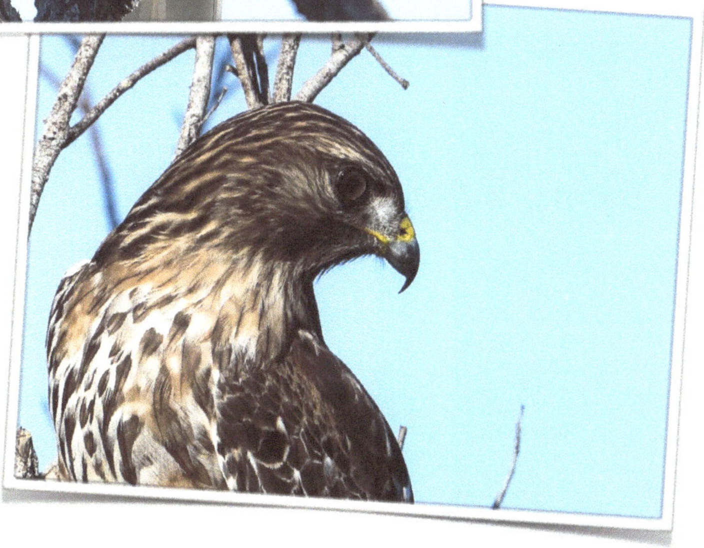

Birds of Prey
Beautiful but vicious killers

The **American bald eagle** has been the national emblem for the United States since 1782. It is majestic, regal, loving and fearsome. All of the eagles photos were taken in southwest Florida mostly at the Pritchett eagle site where Harriet and her mate M15 reside.

The **osprey** is often referred to as the sea hawk because it has a ferocious appetite for fish. The osprey photos were taken at Blue Cypress Lake and Pine Island in Florida.

The **hawk** is an avid hunter of insects, rodents and frogs. Photos of the hawks were taken in North Fort Myers and Naples in Florida.

As cute as they are, the **burrowing owls** are very efficient in hunting down their preys. All of their photos were taken in Cape Coral, Florida where they are the city's official bird.

The **crested caracara** is a bird of prey. Their photos in this book were taken in May of 2019 on the Dutch Antilles Island of Bonaire.

American Bald Eagle

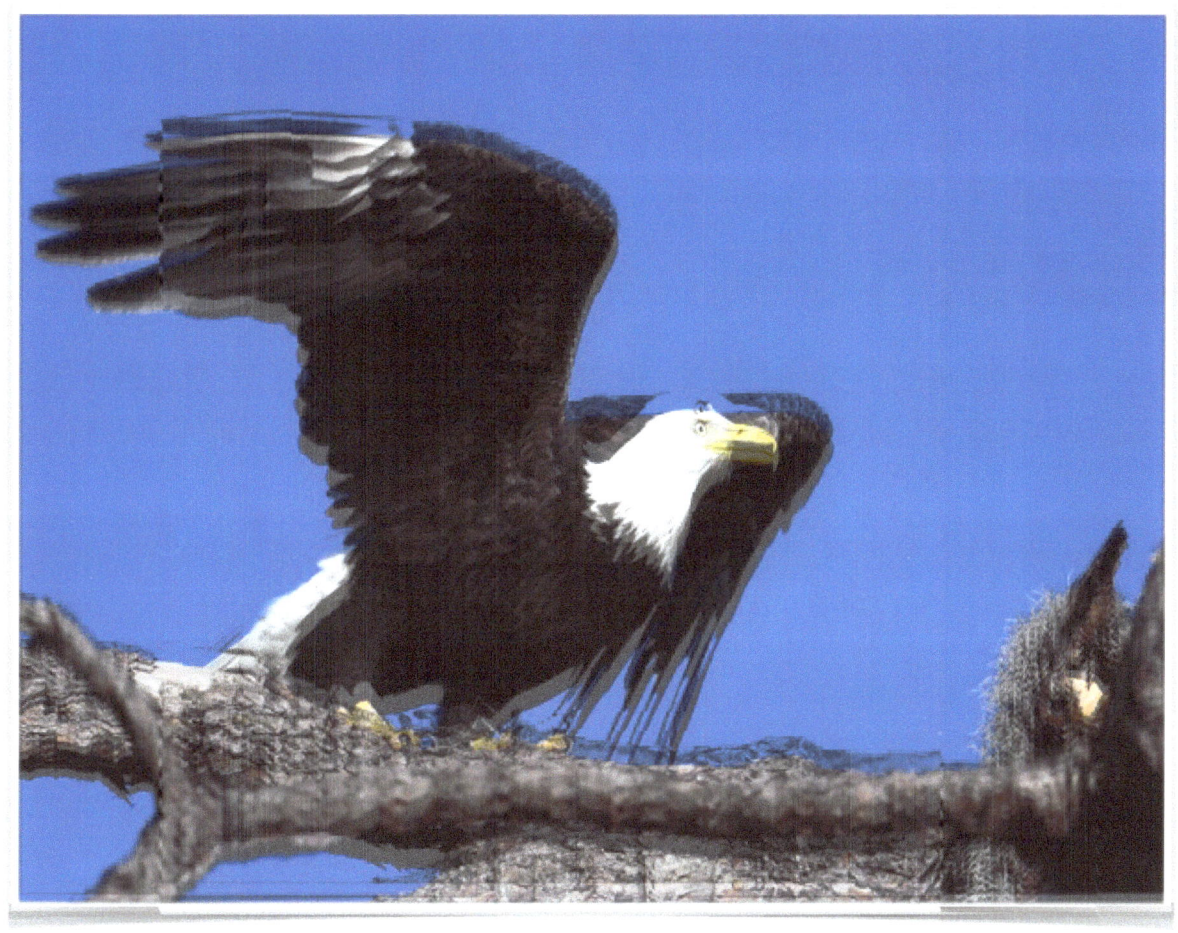

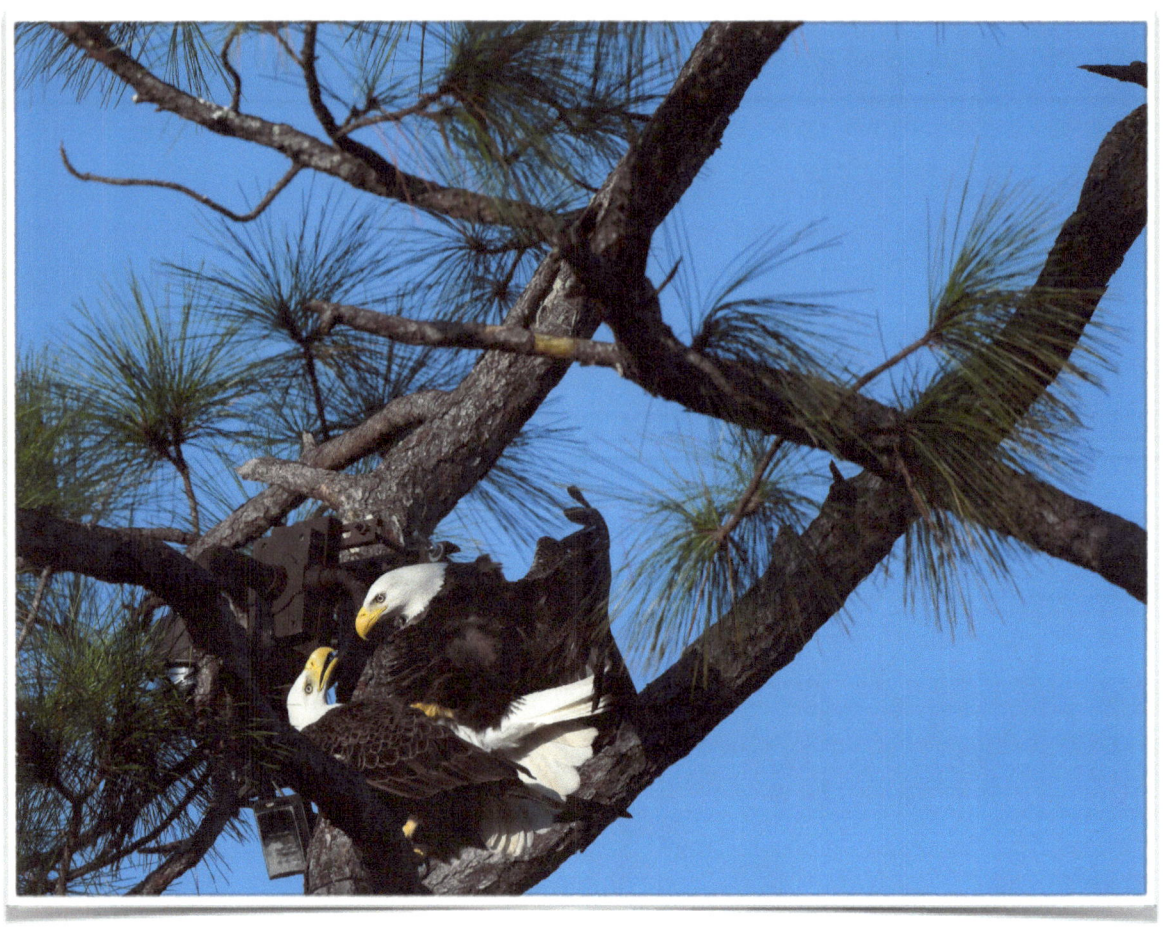
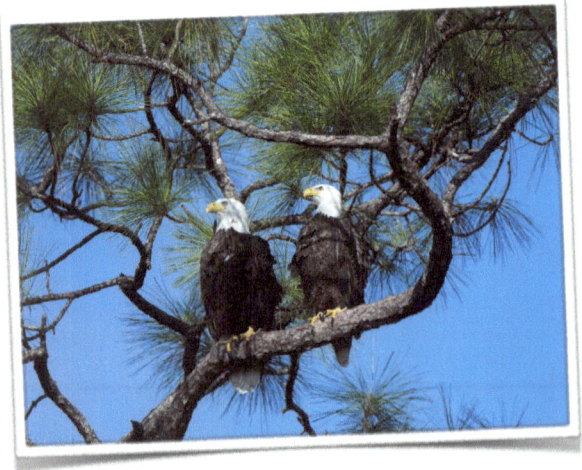
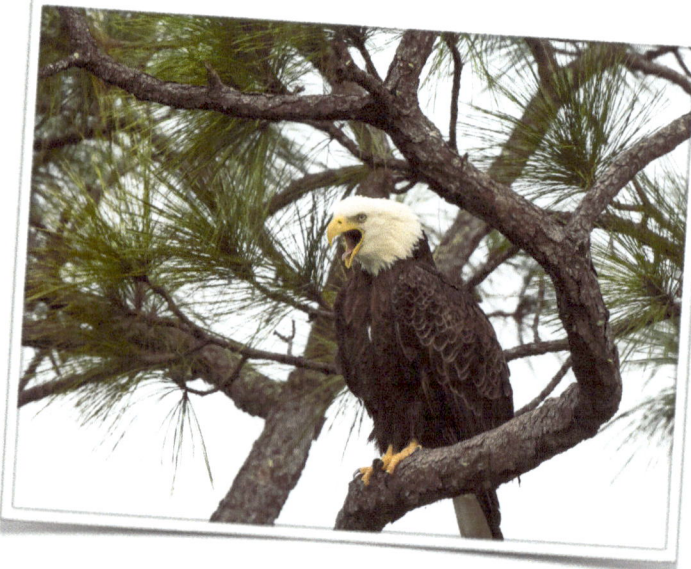

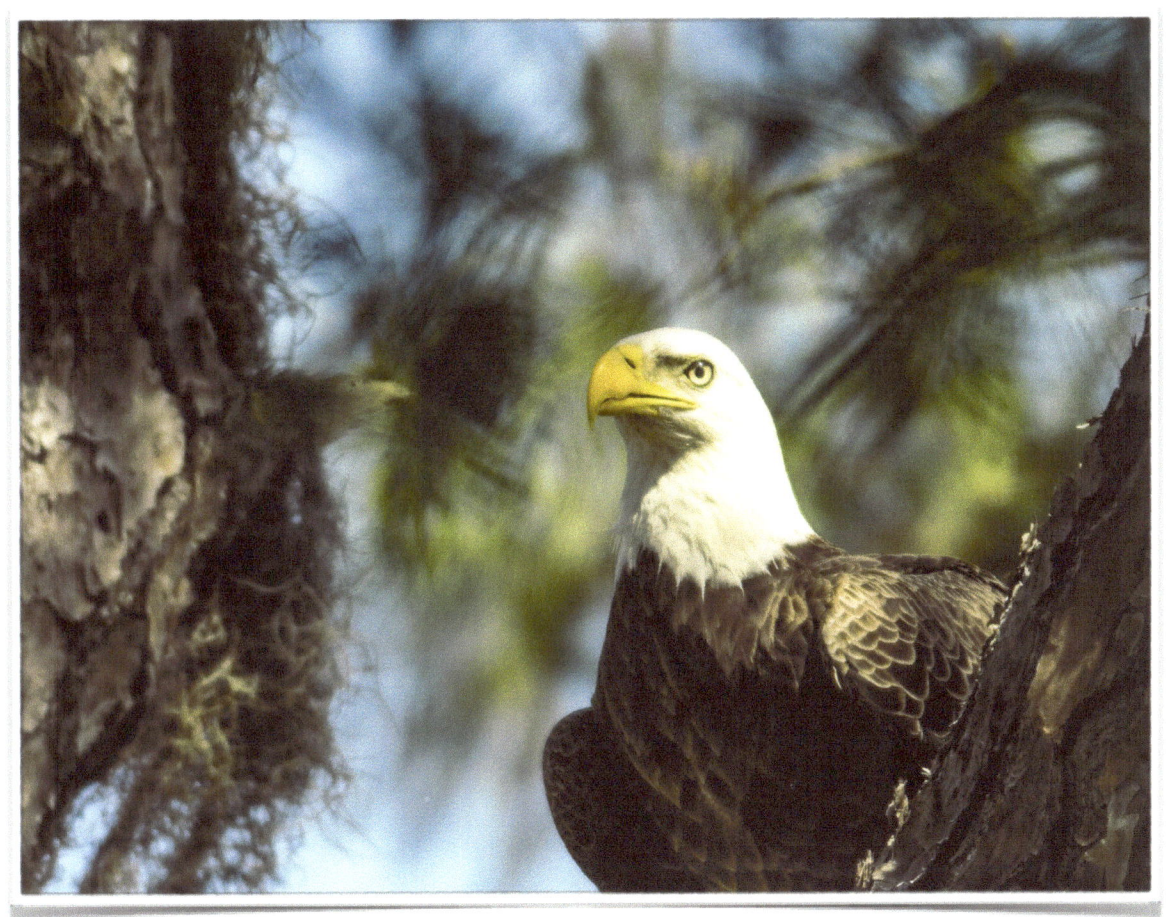
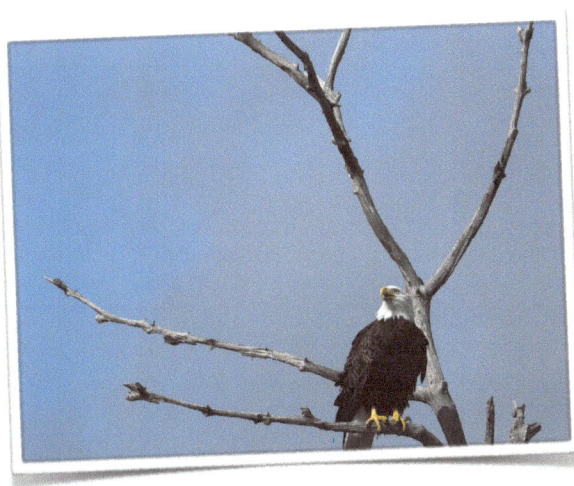
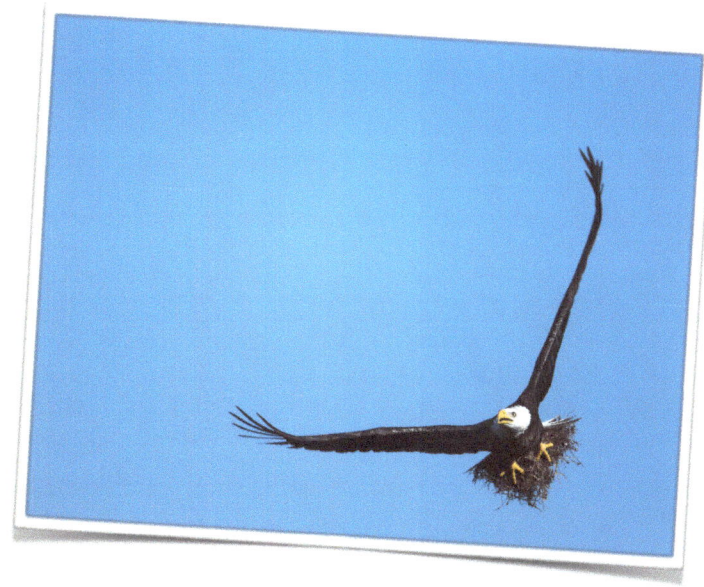

Birds of prey, Page 5

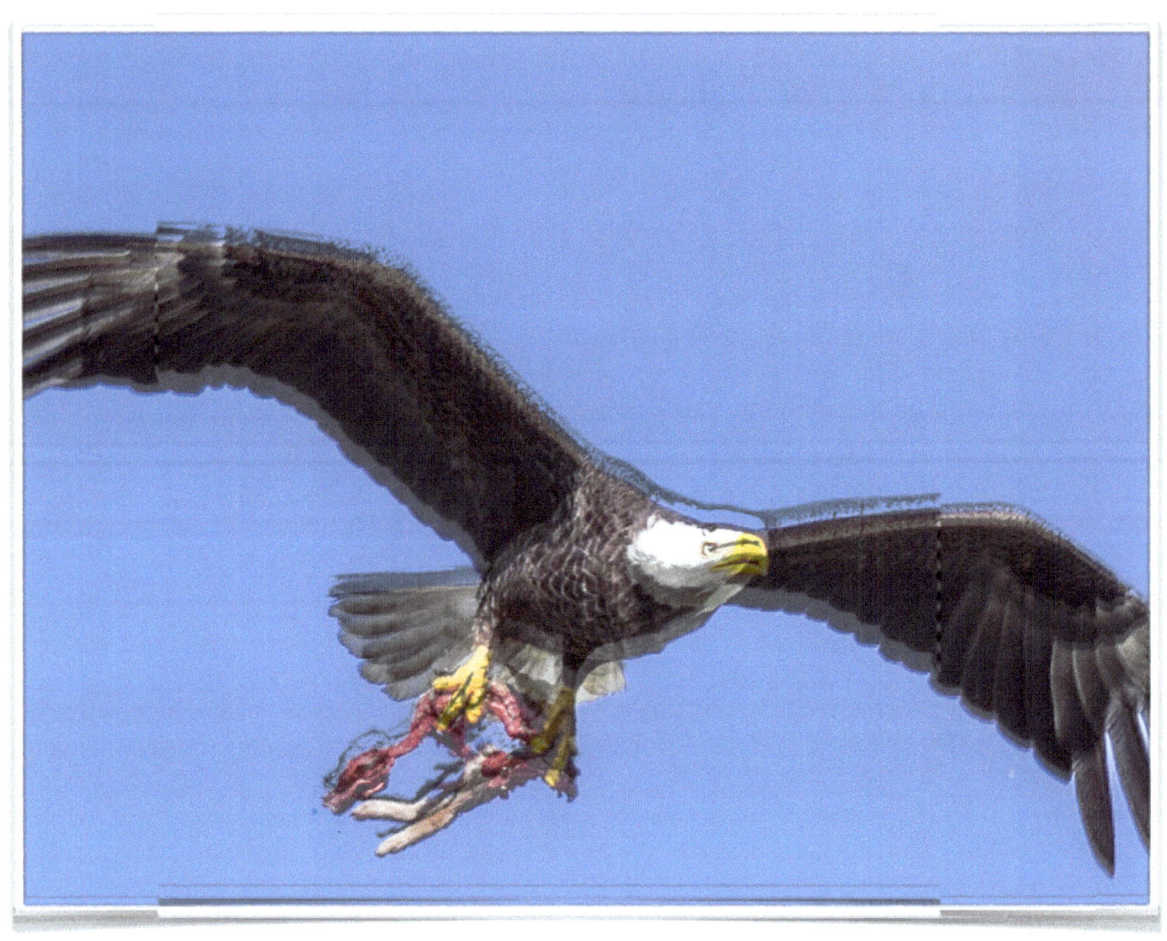
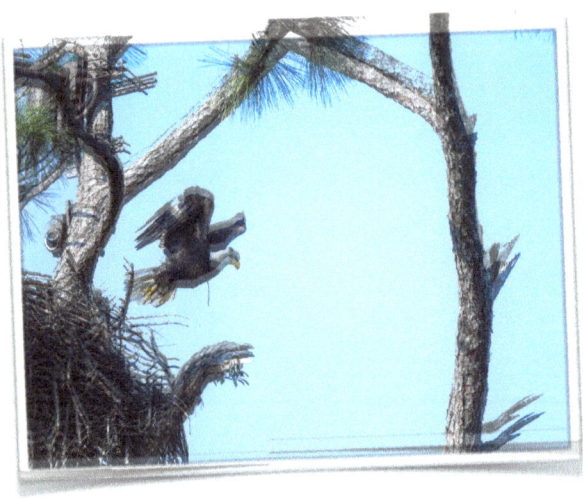
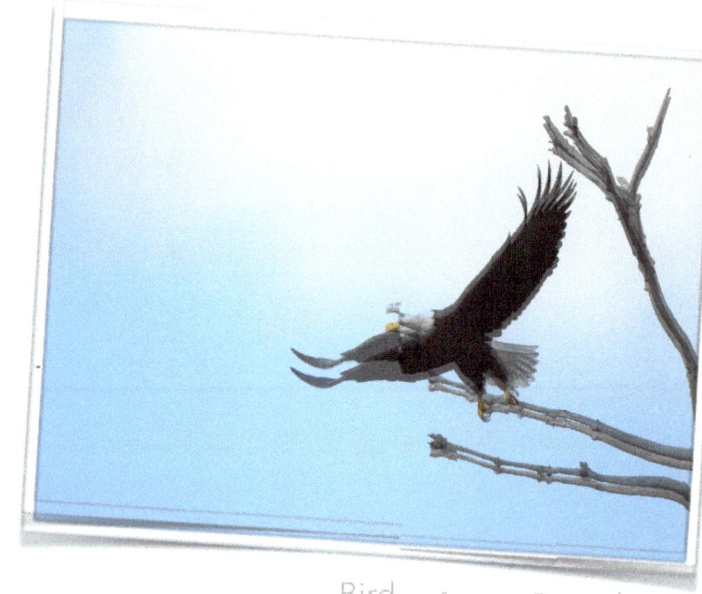

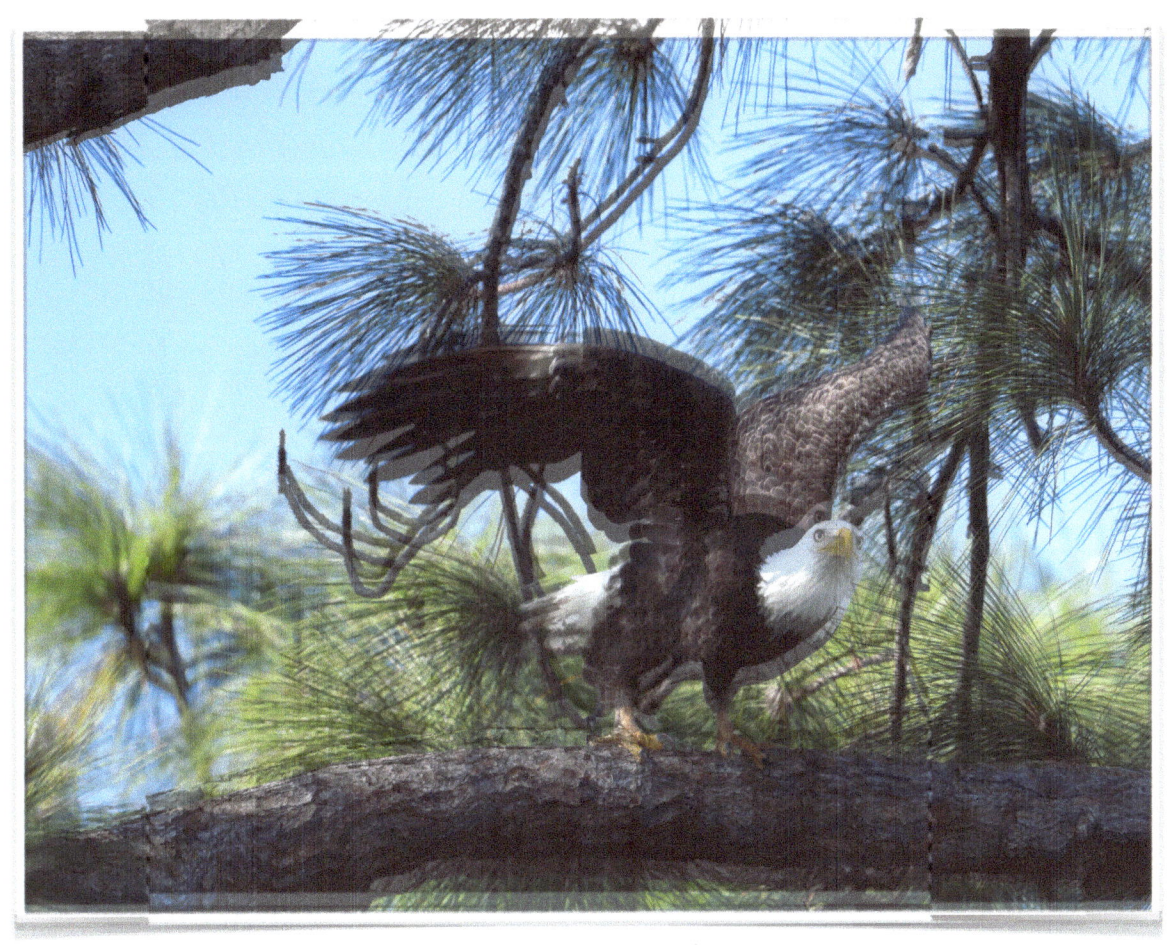
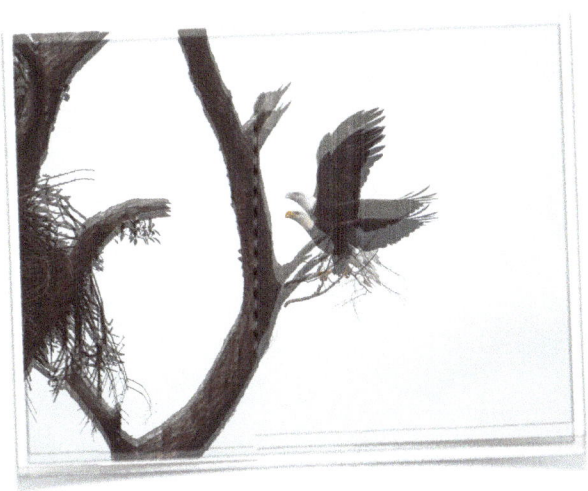
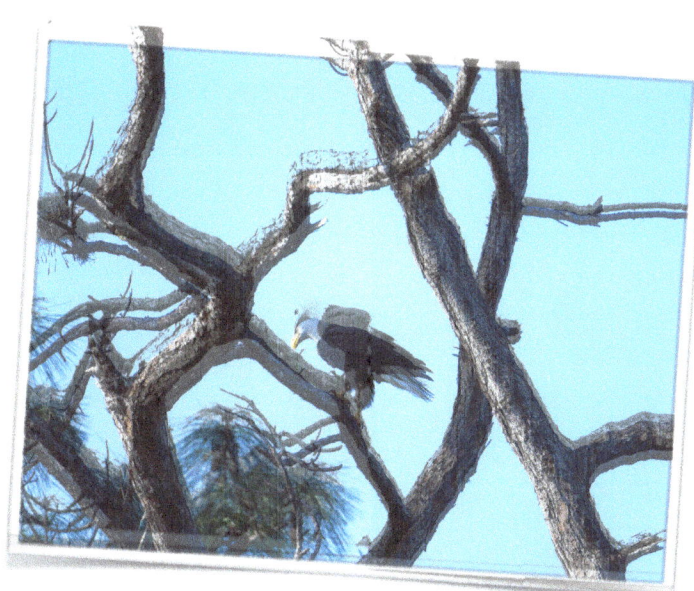

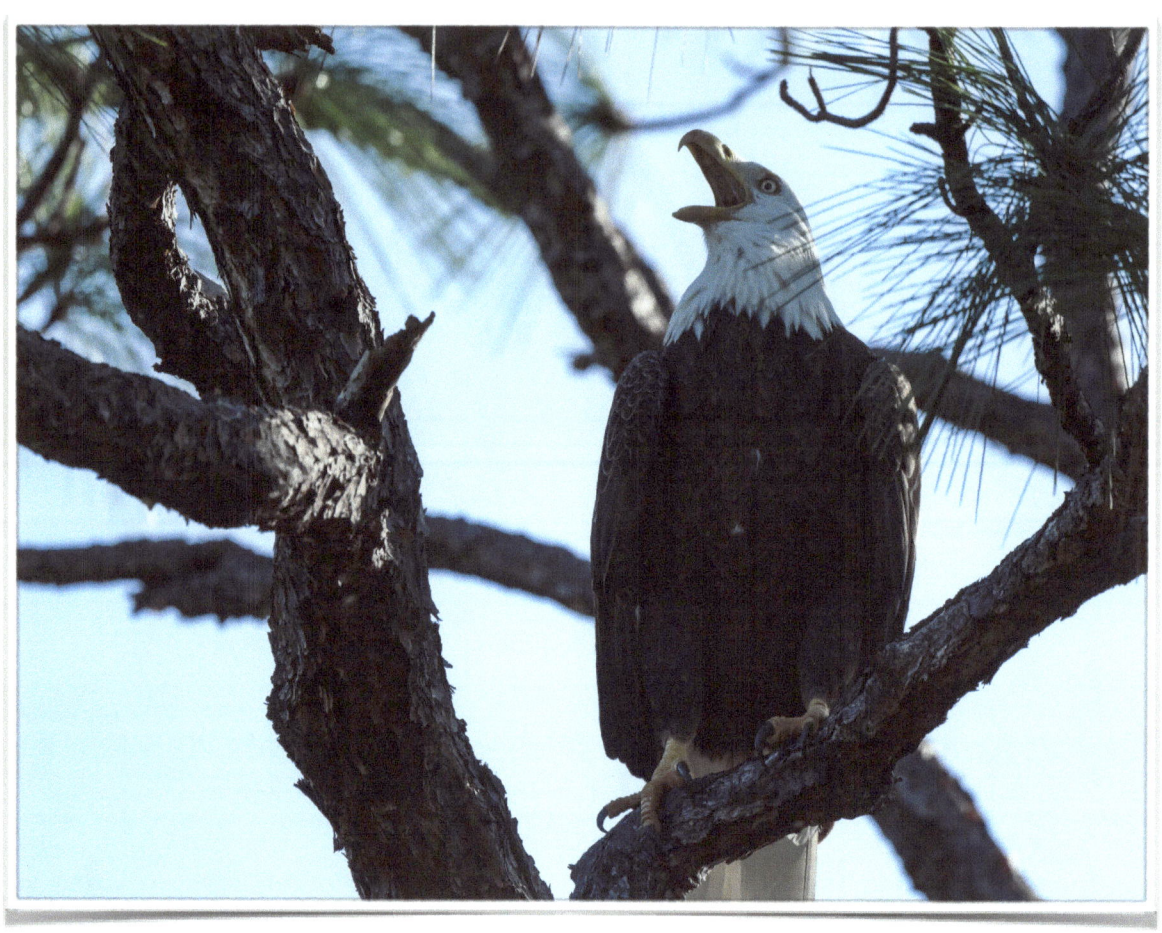
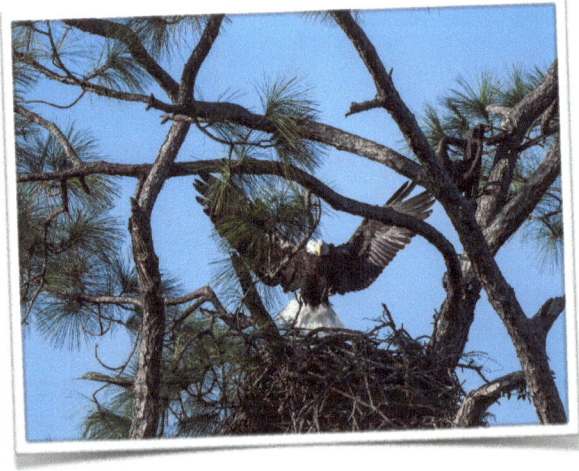
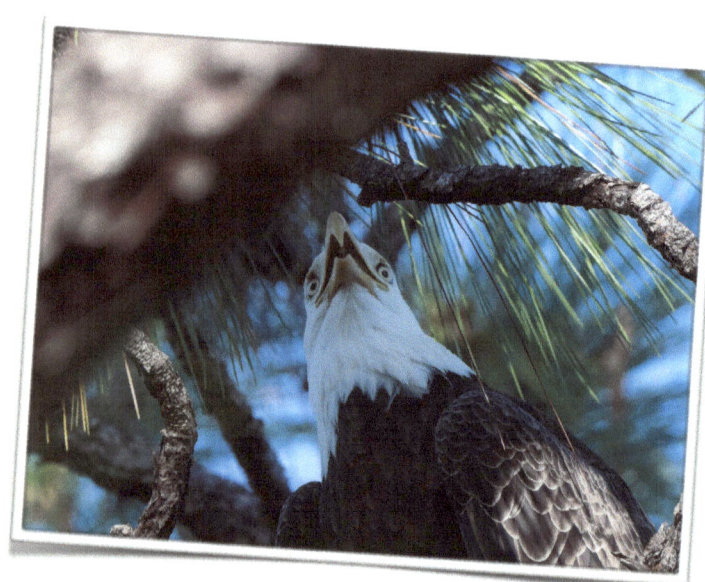

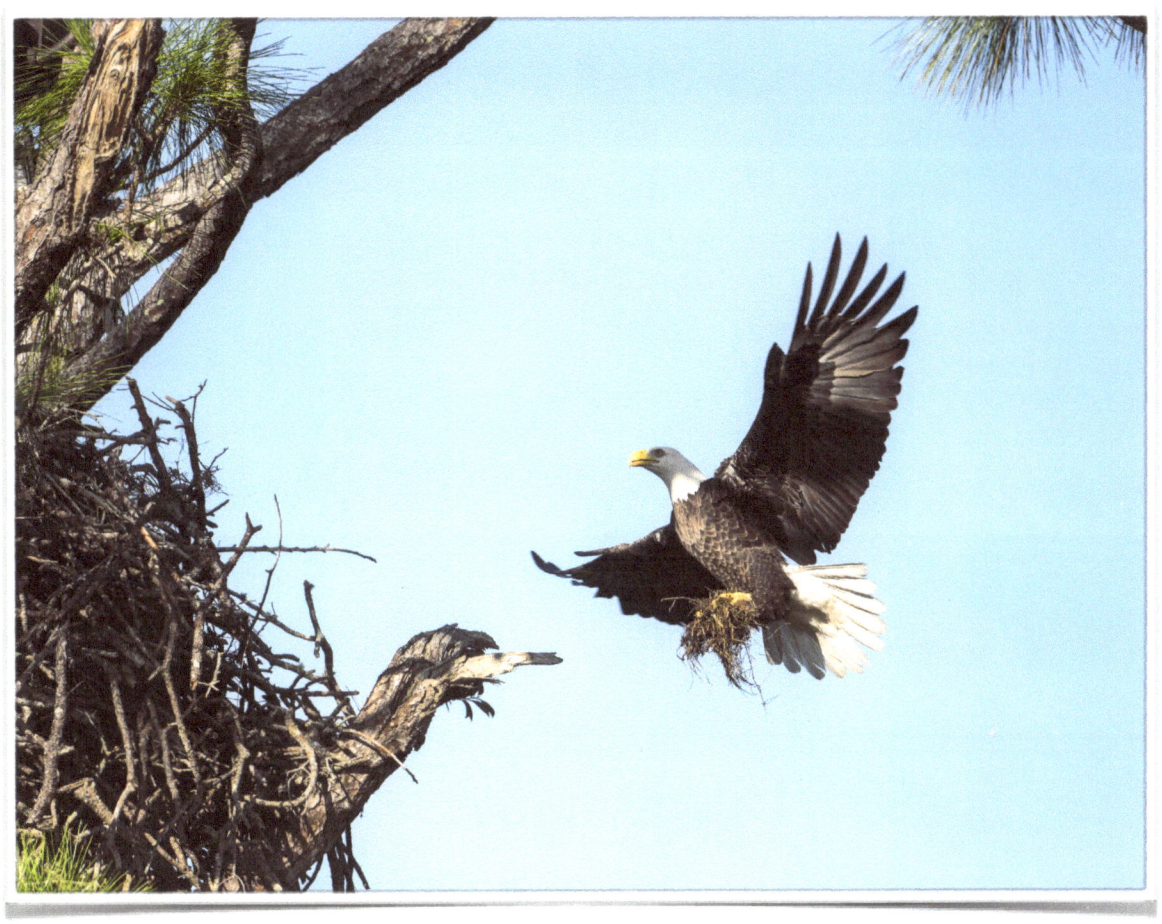
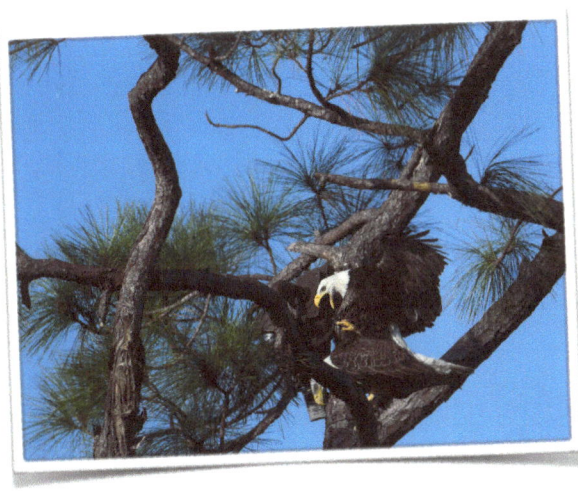
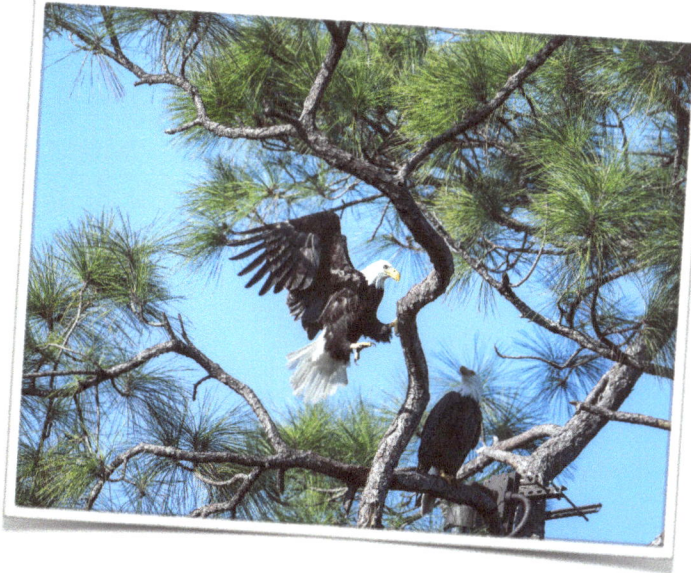

Ospreys

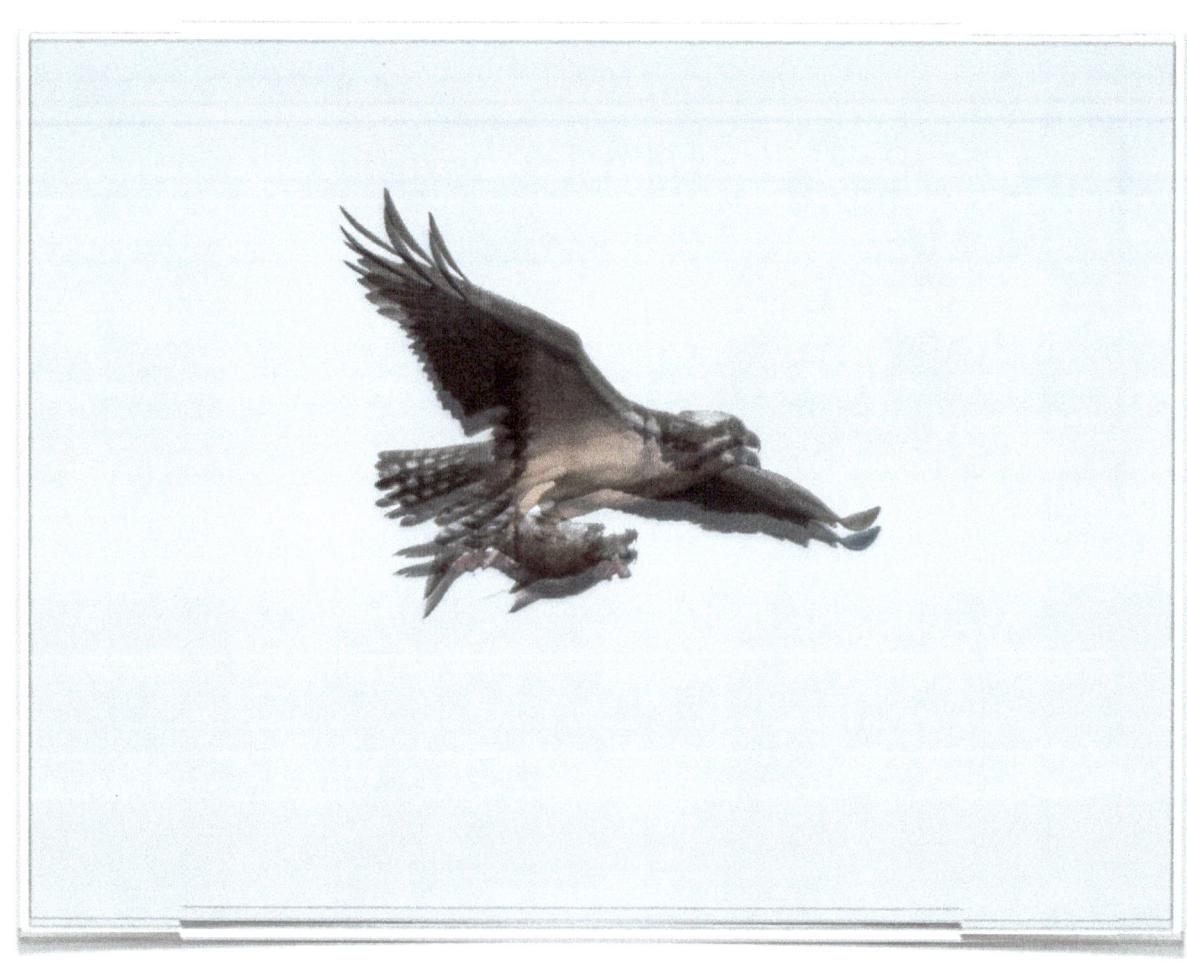

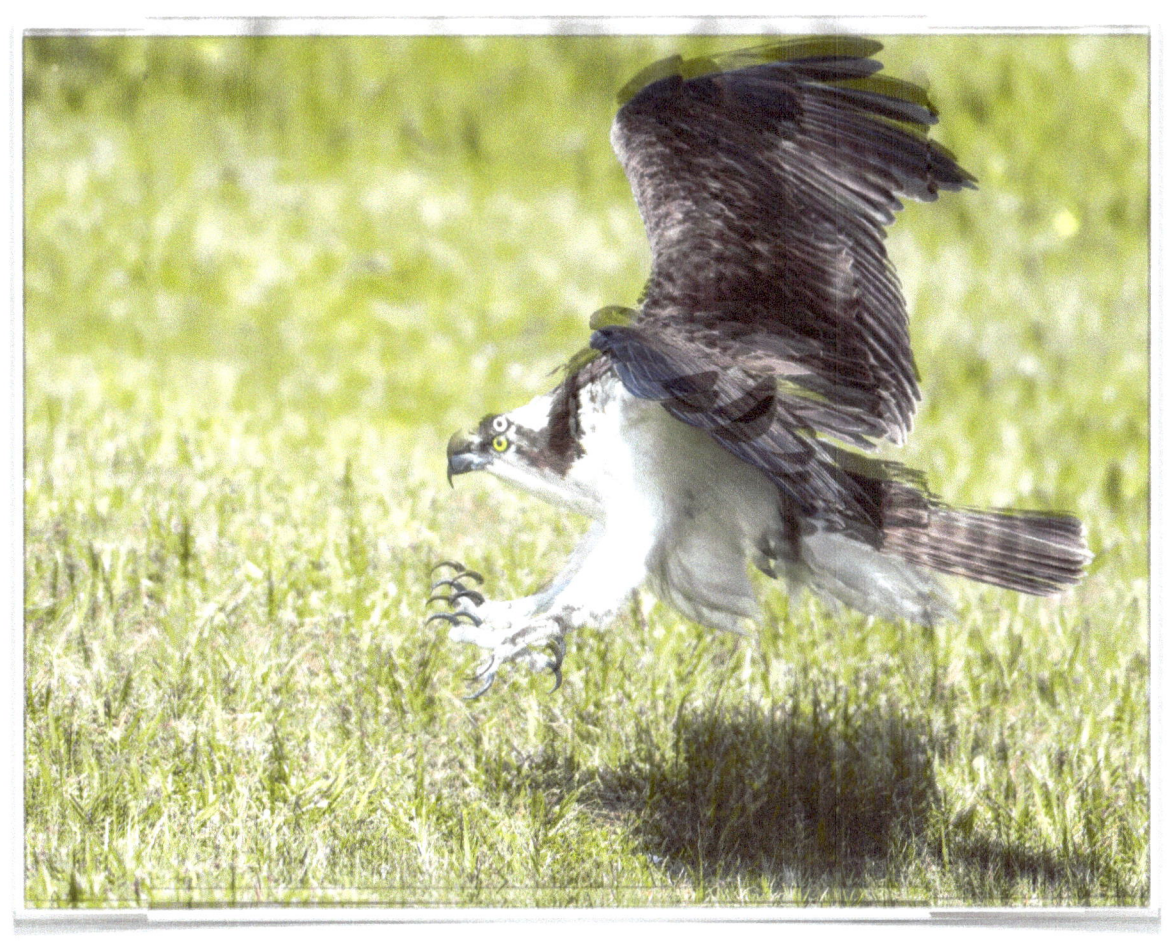
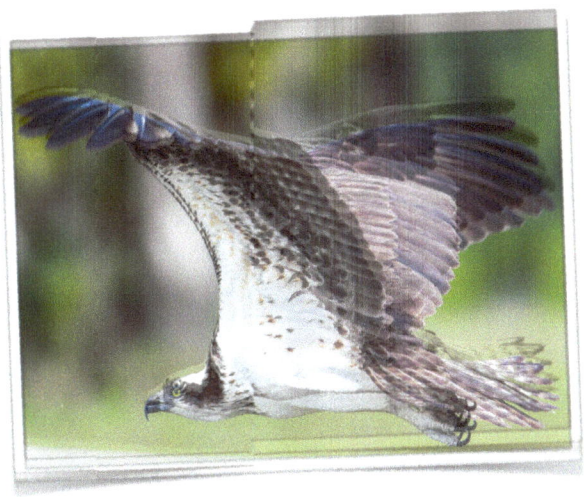
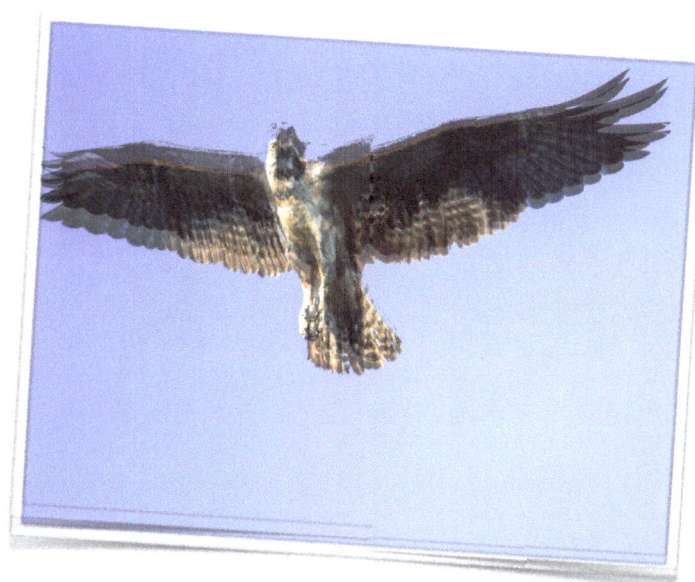

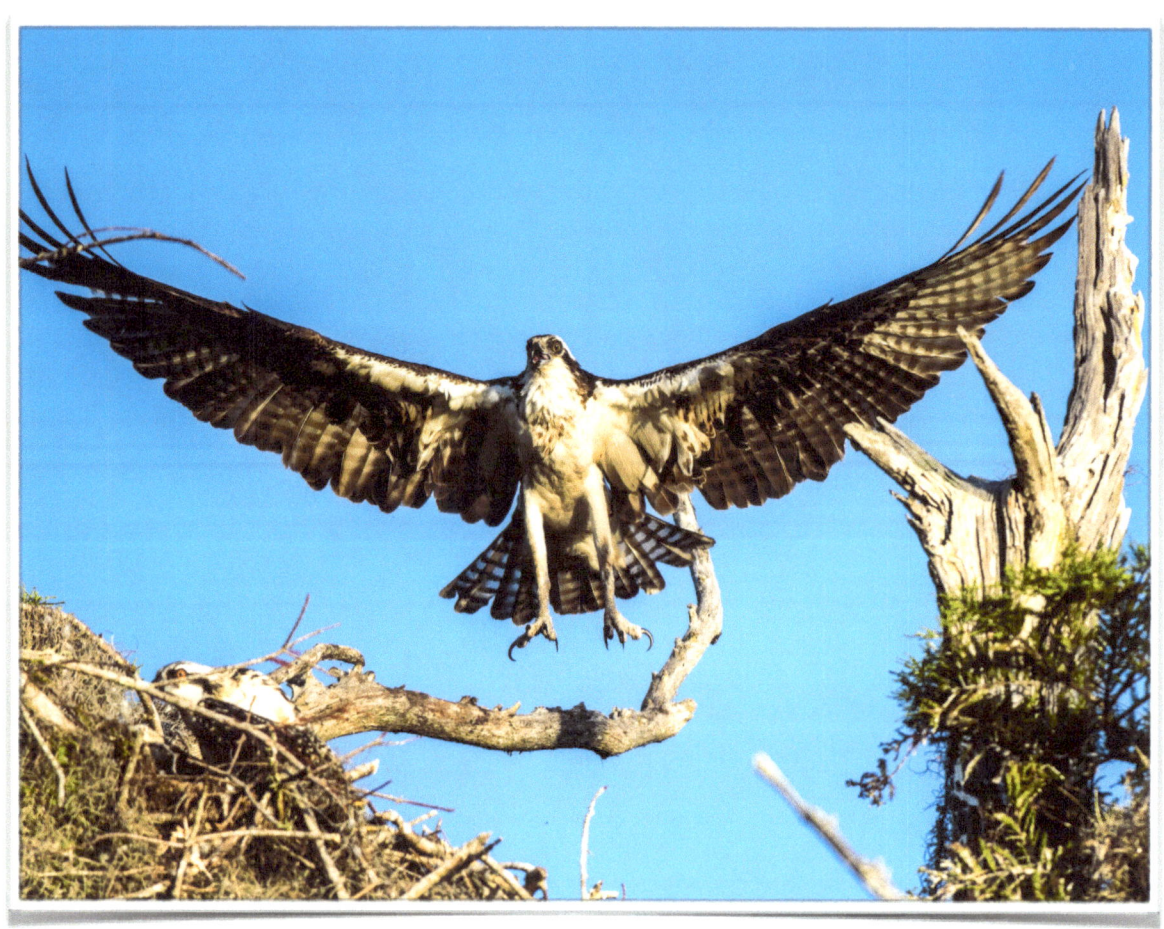
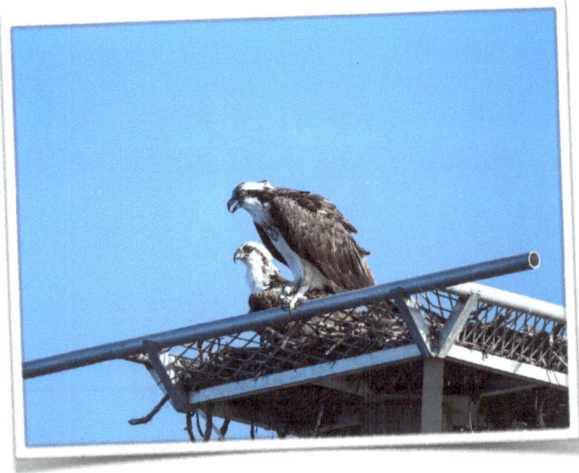
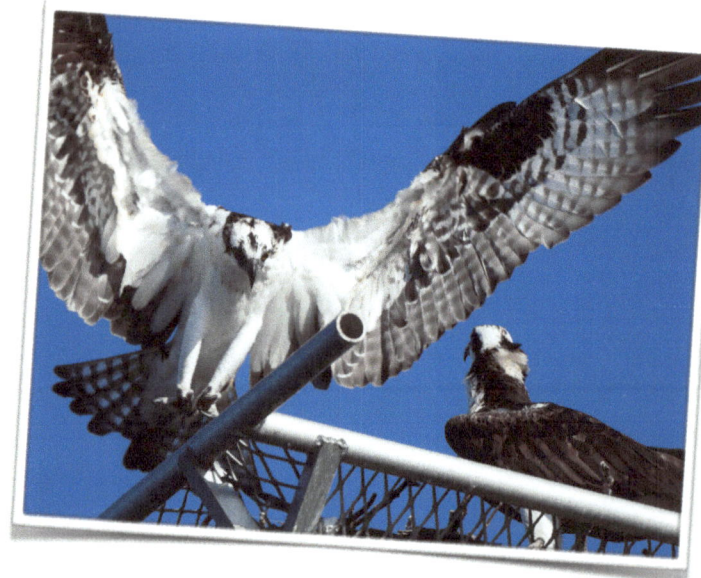

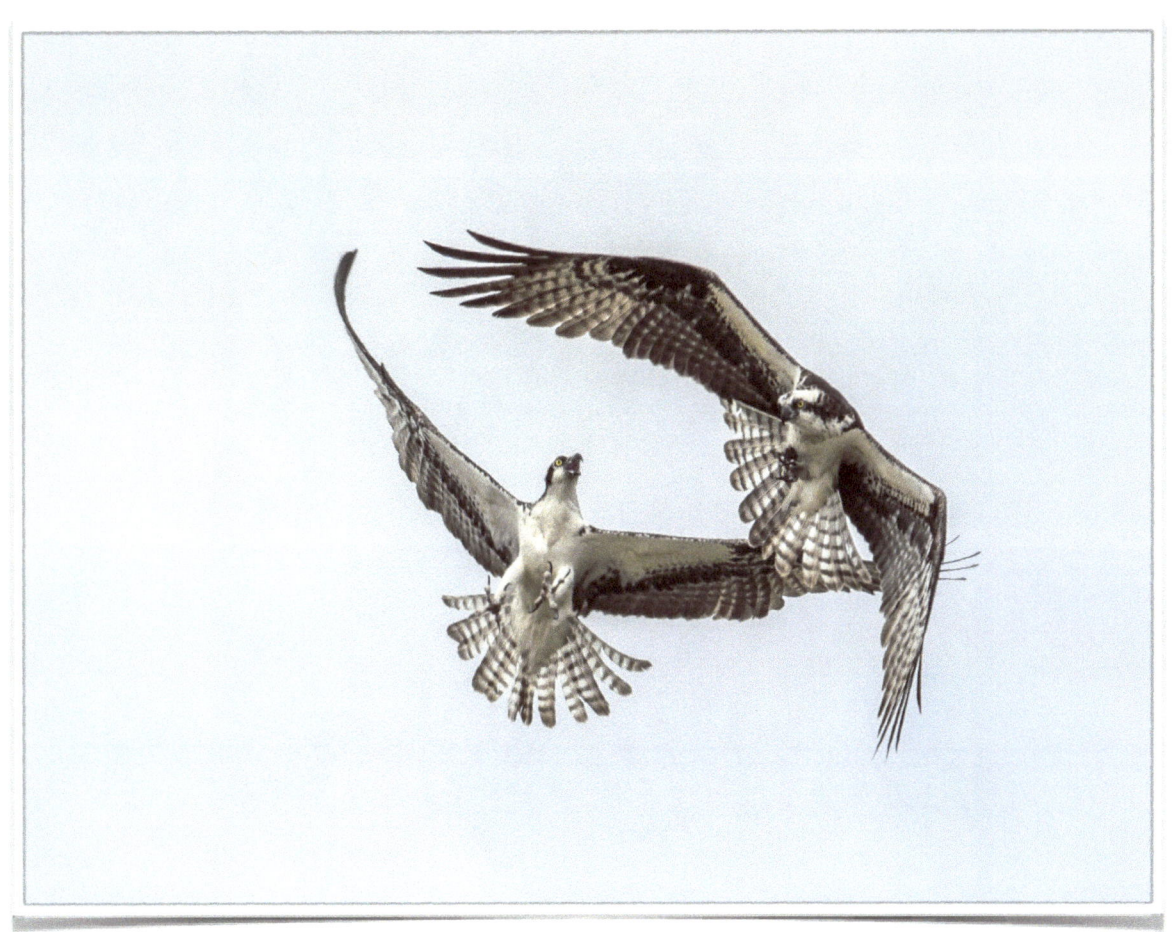
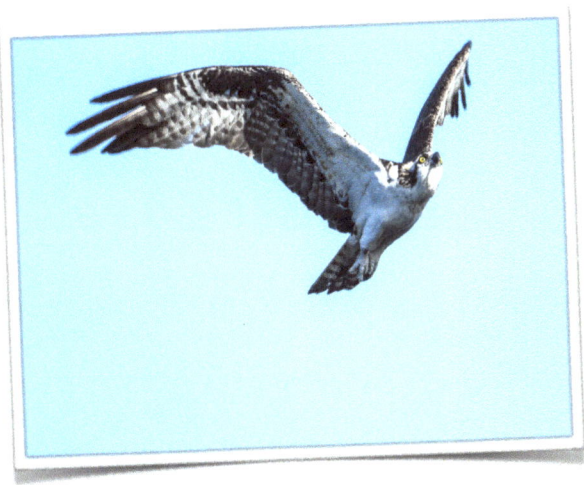
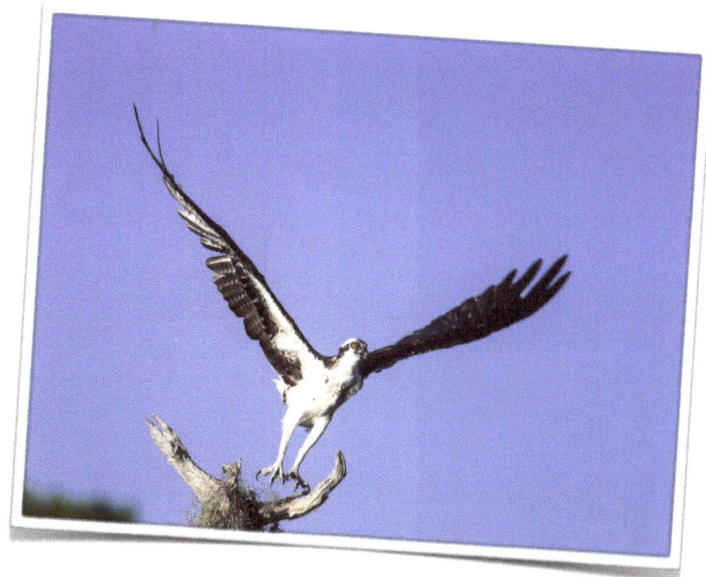

Birds of prey, Page 13

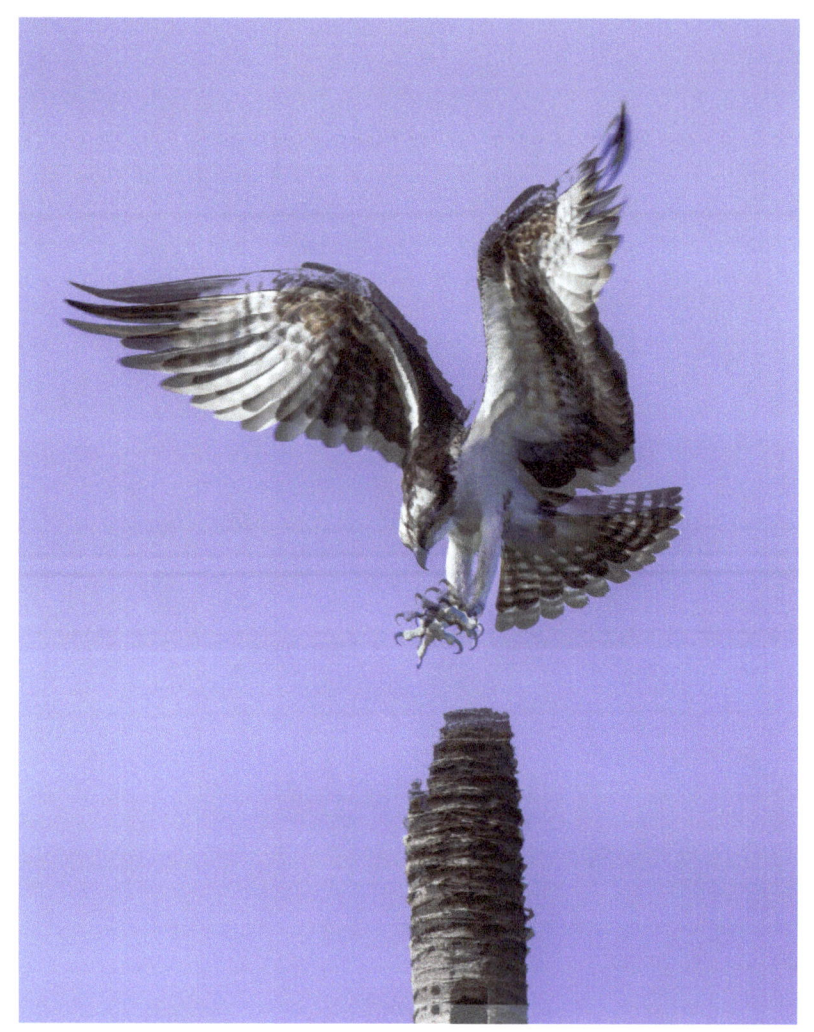
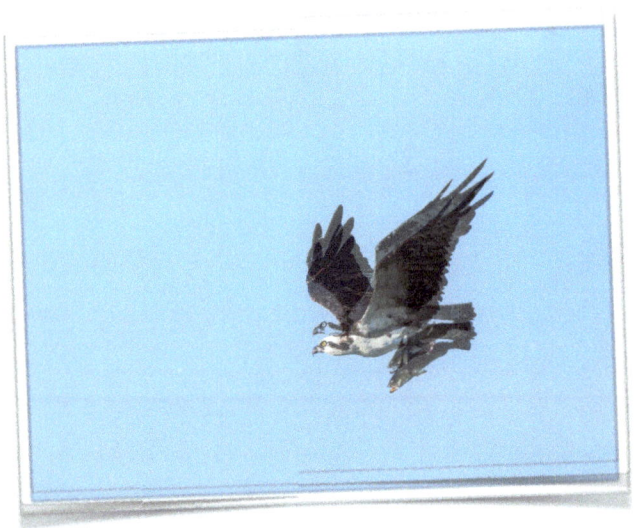
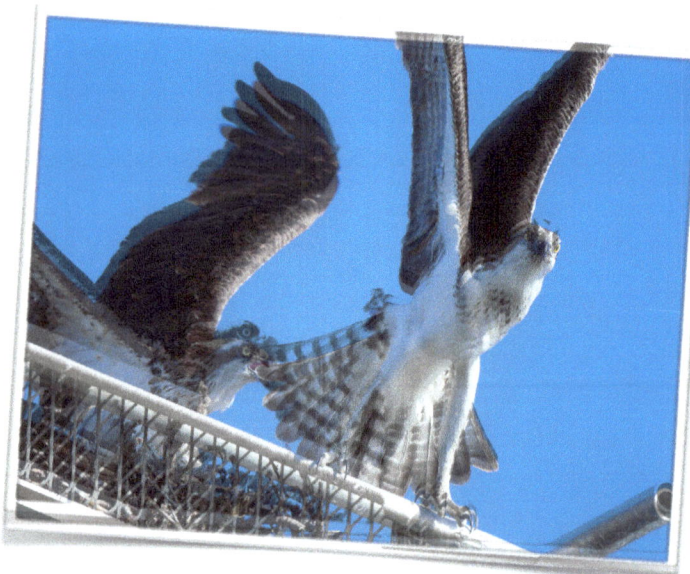

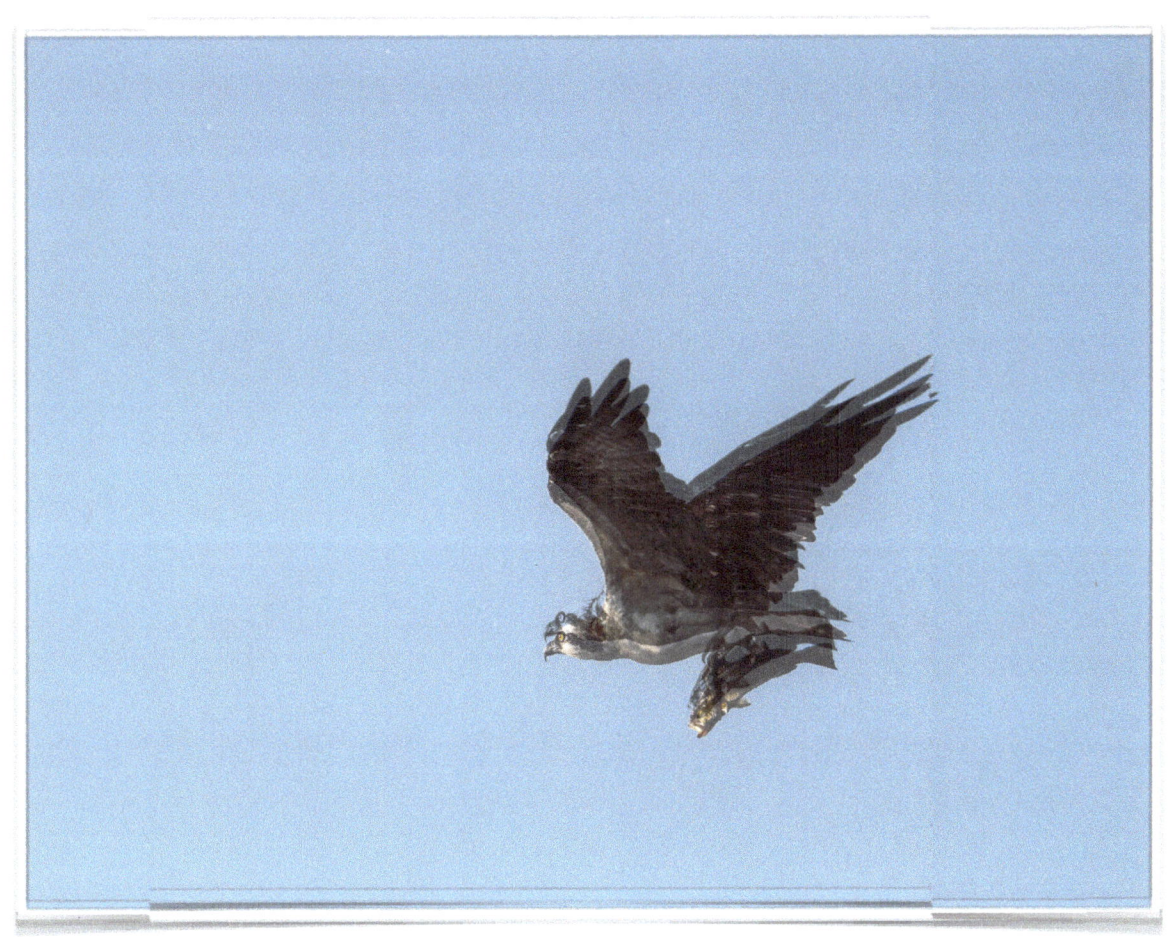
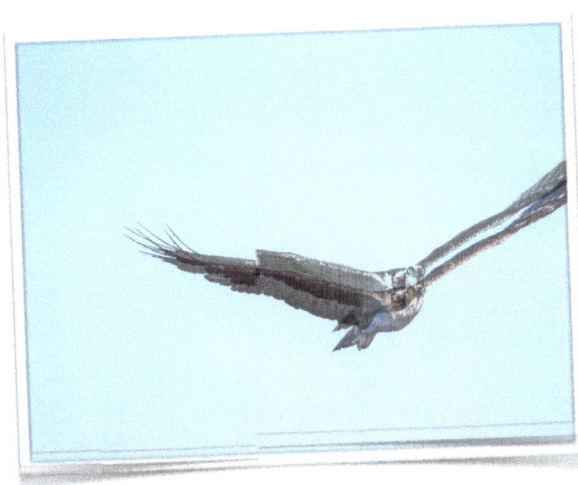
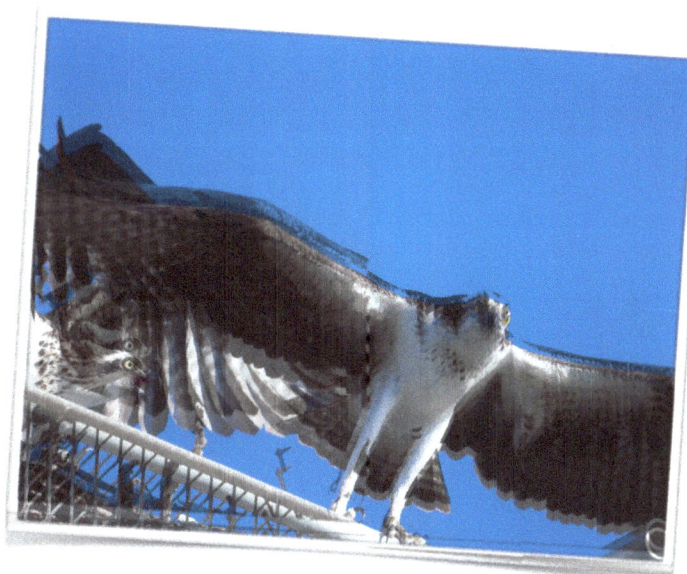

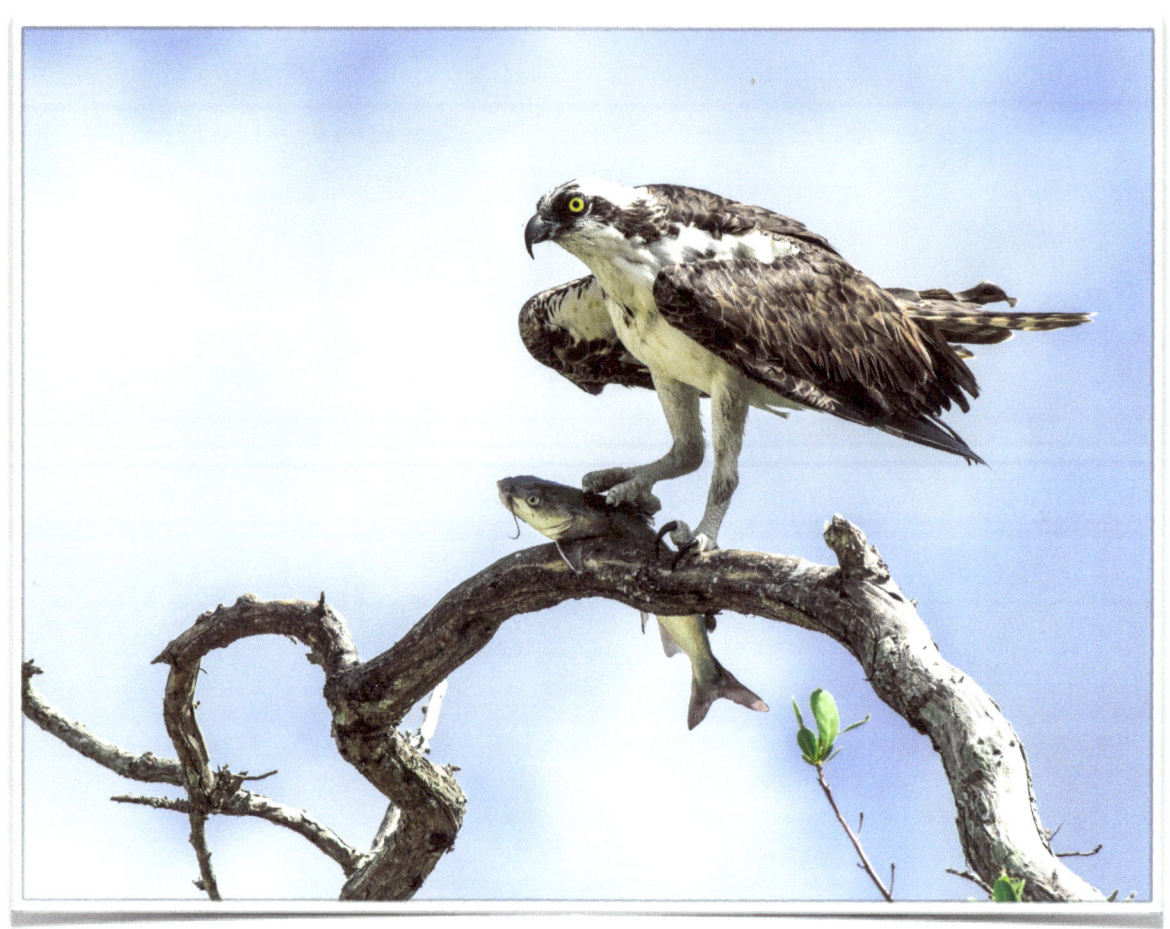
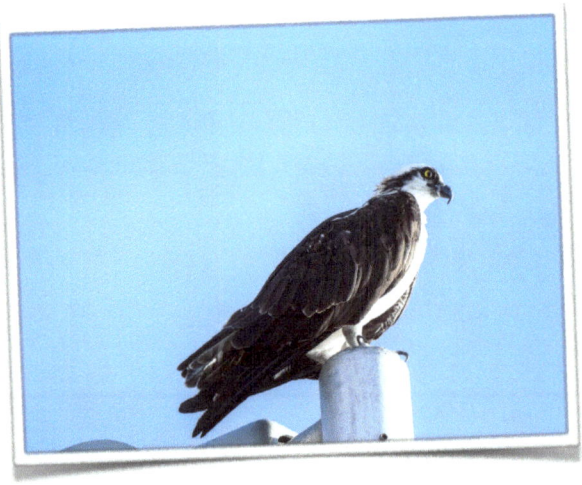
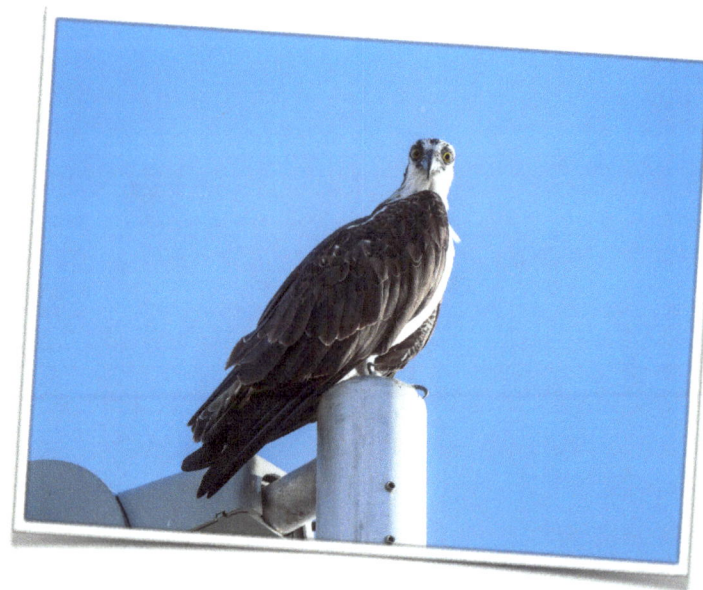

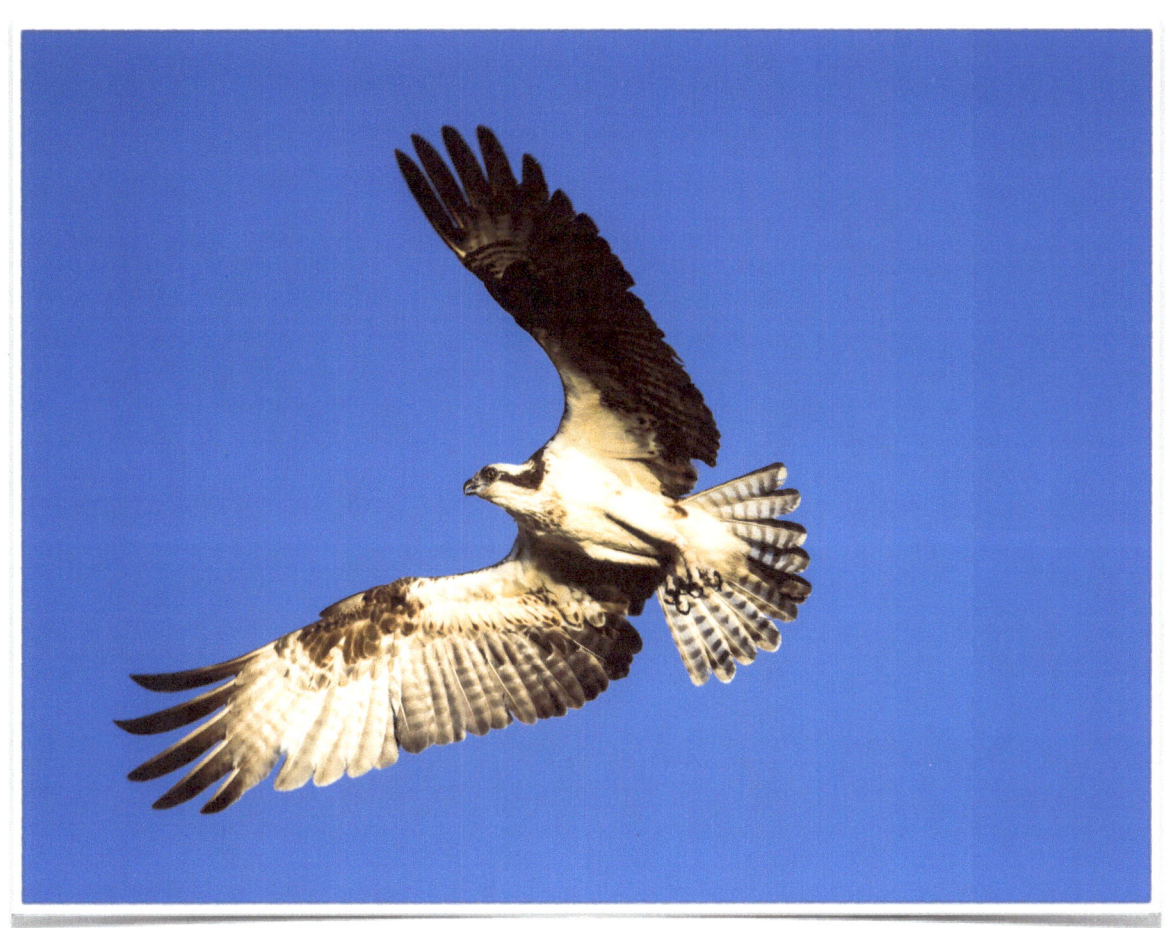
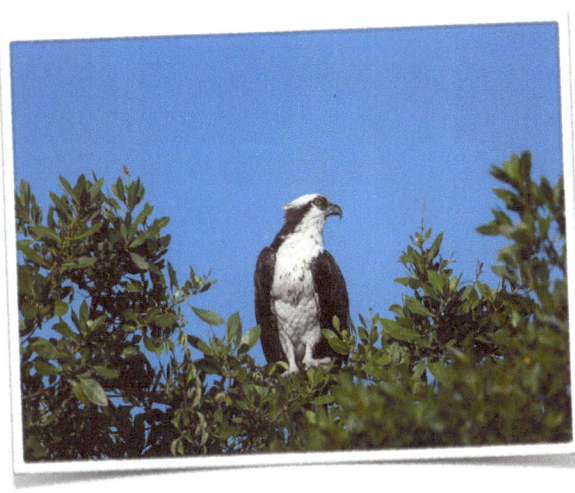
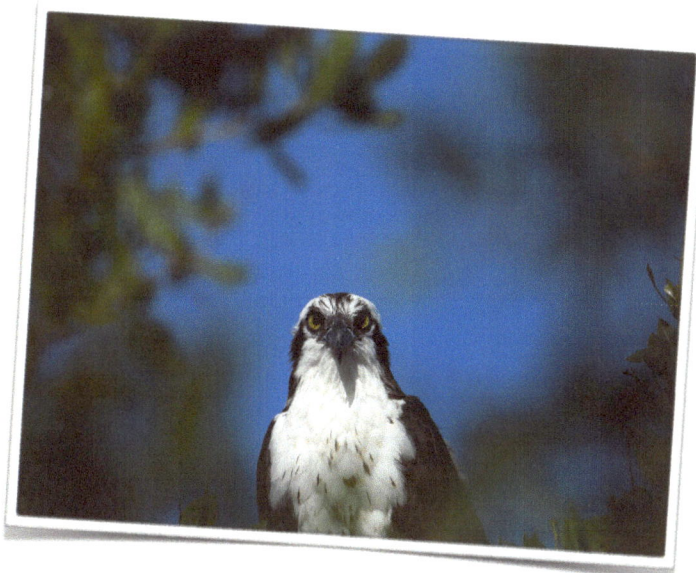

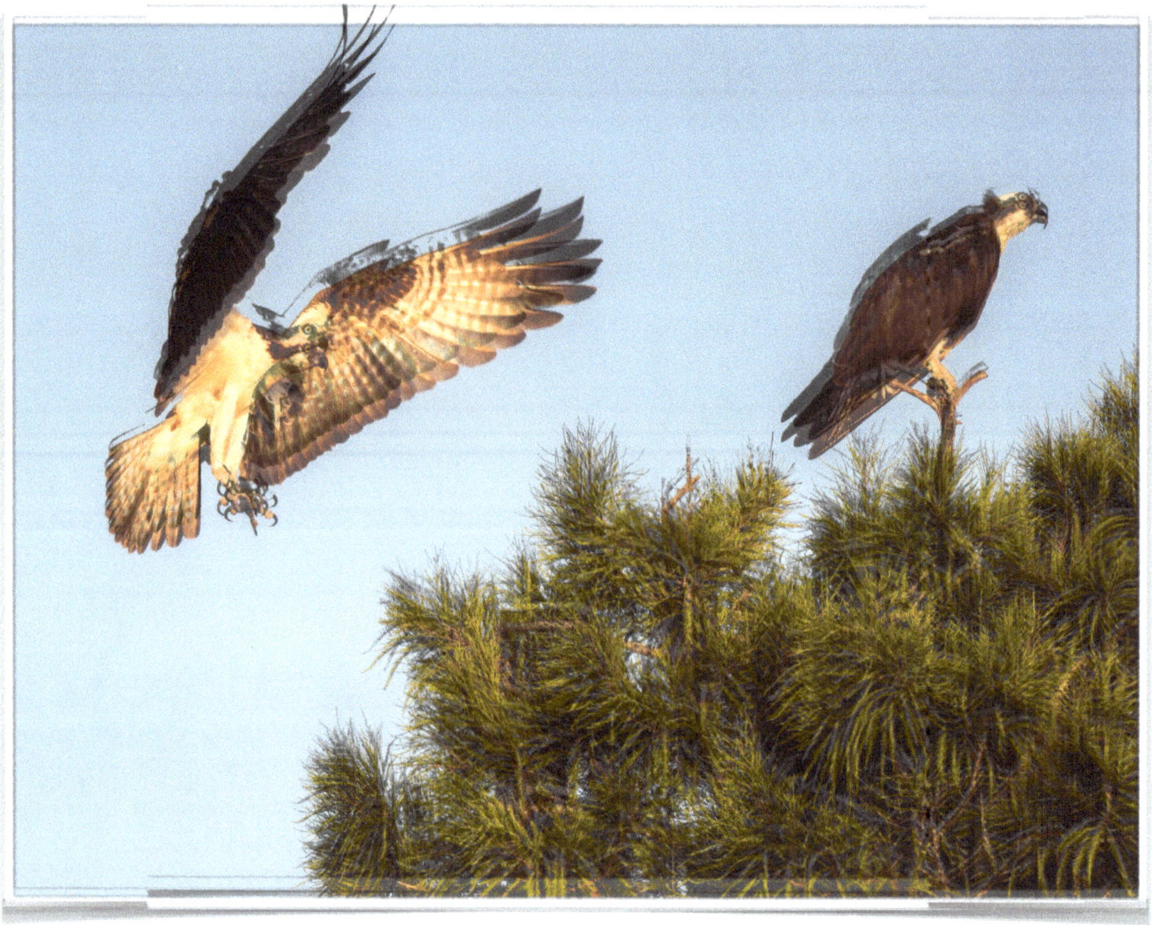

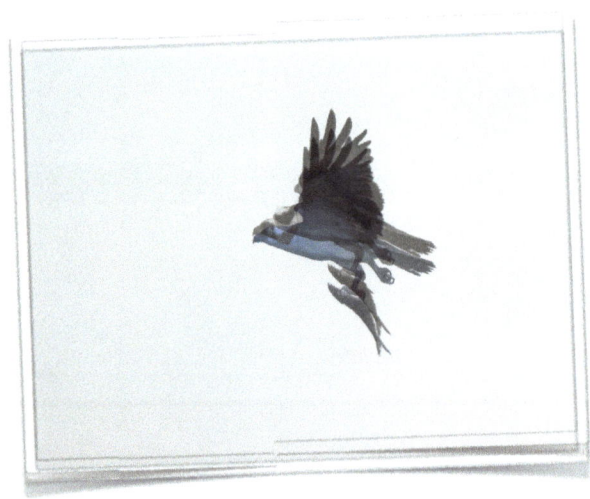
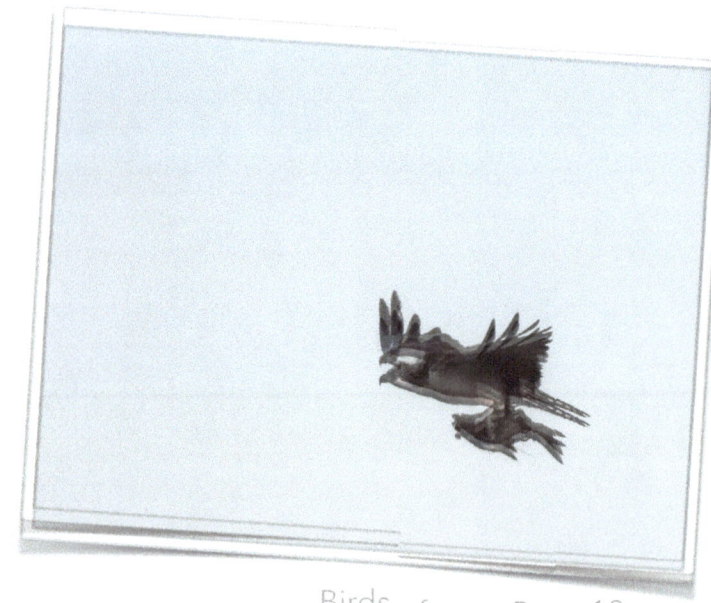

Hawks

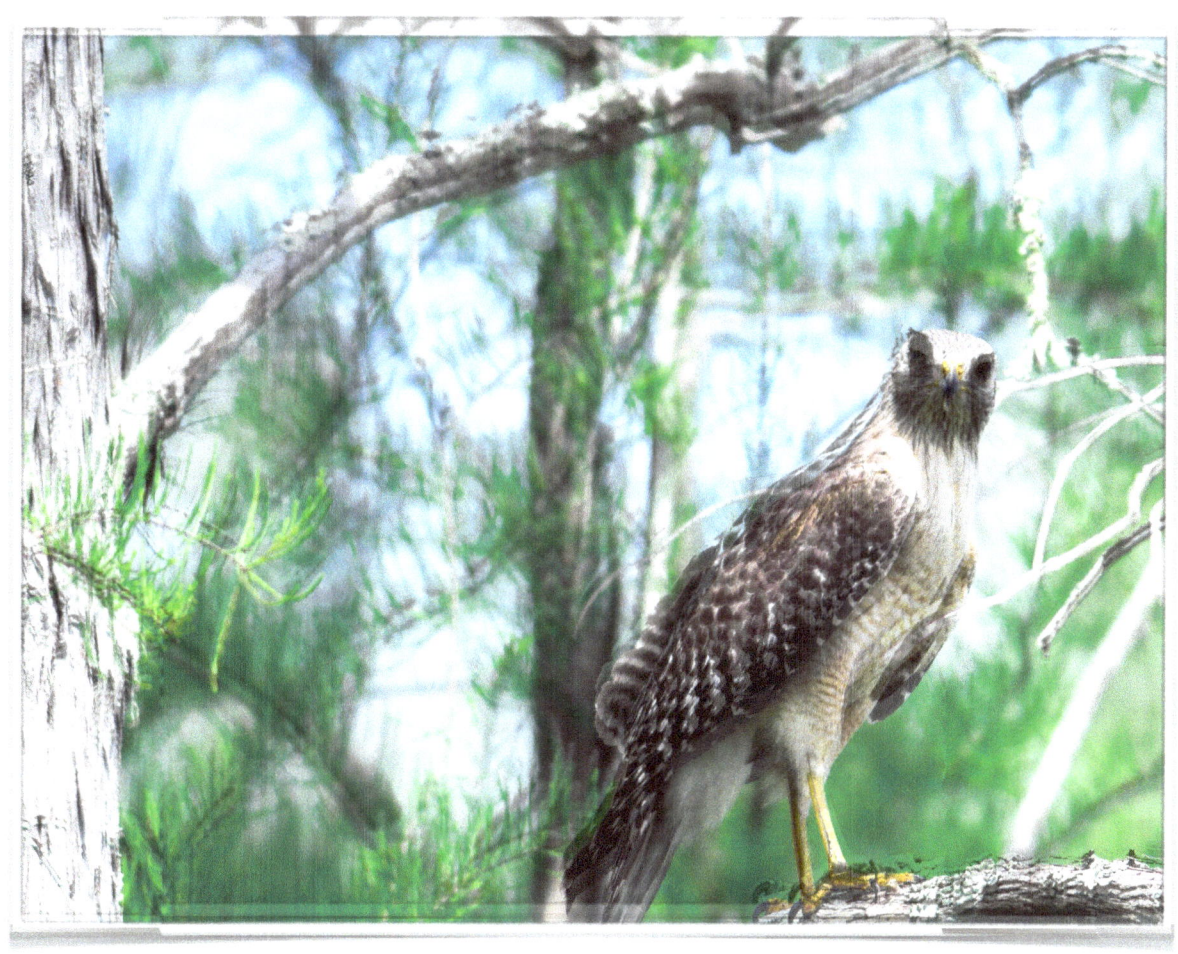

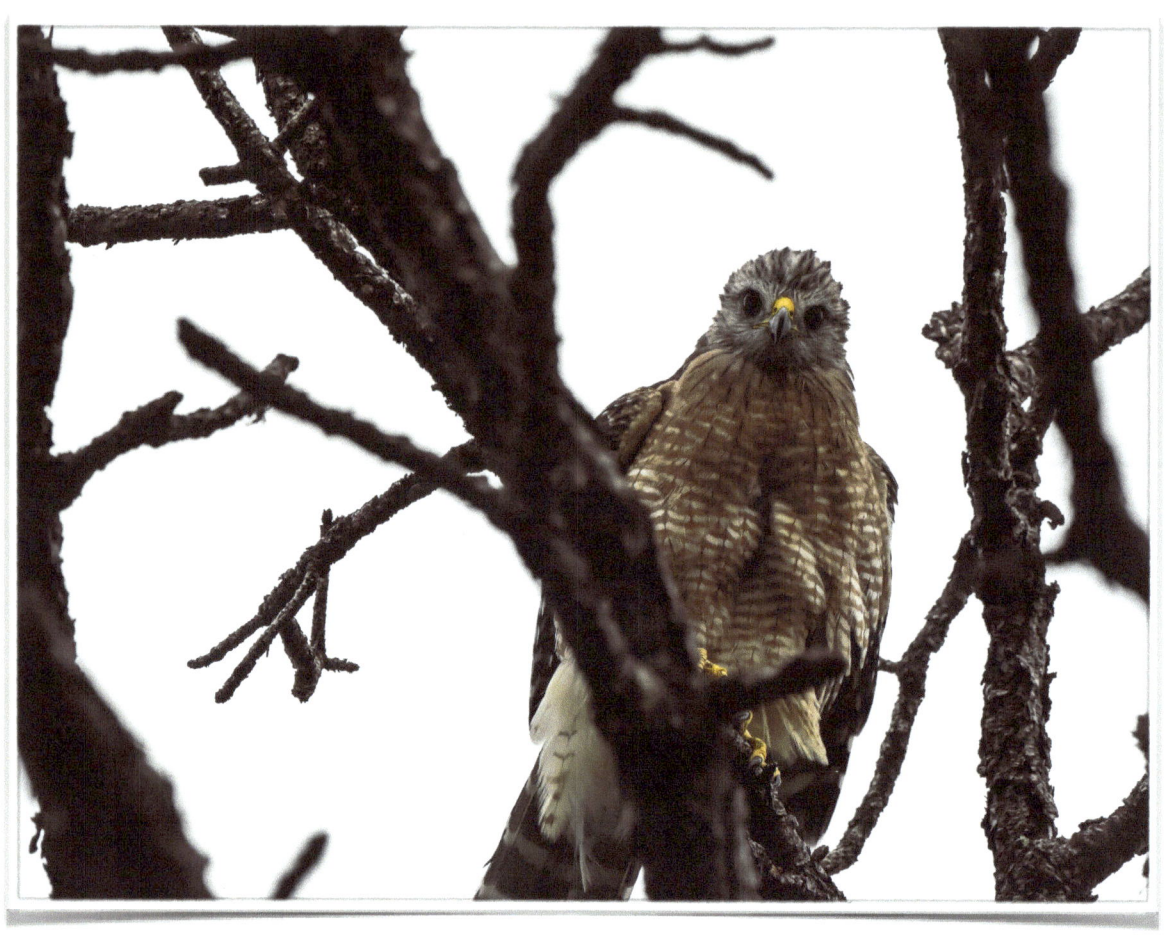
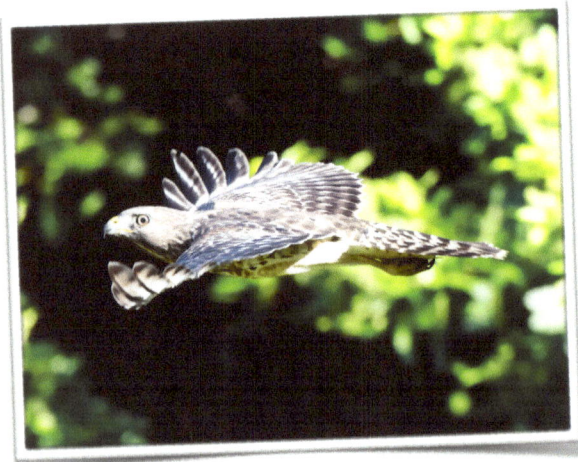
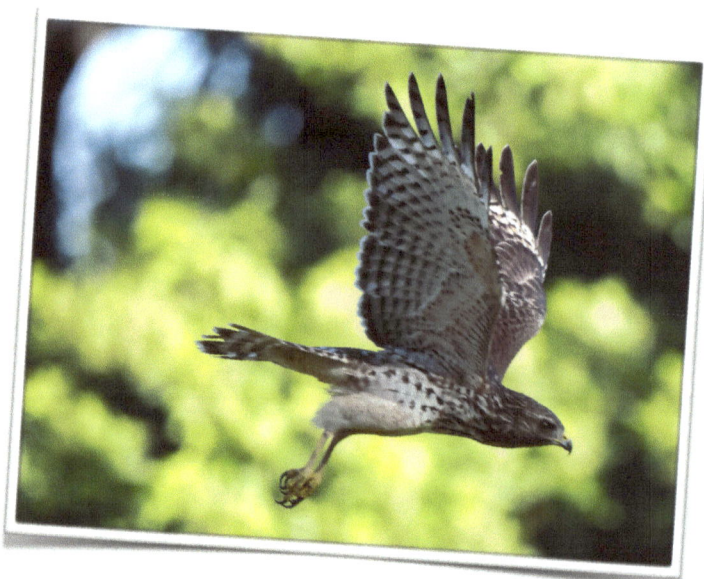

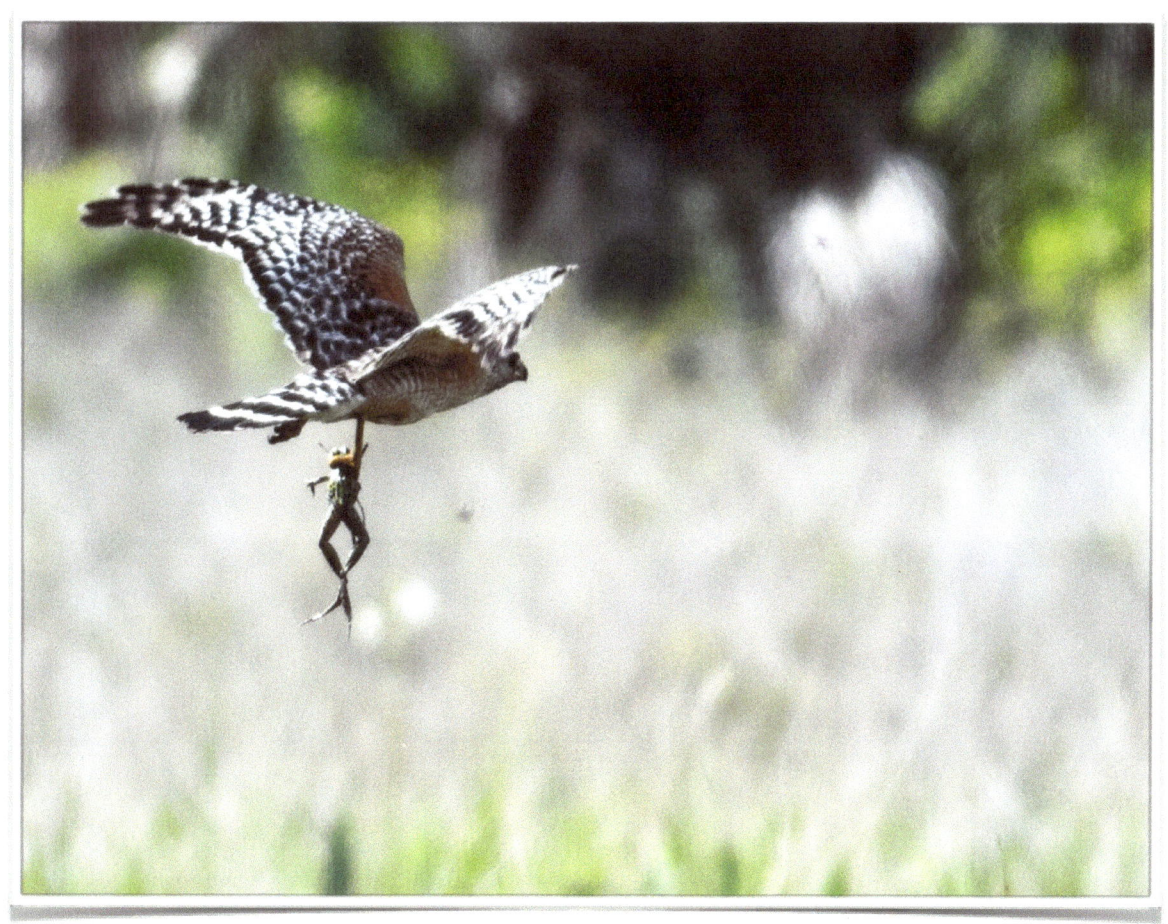
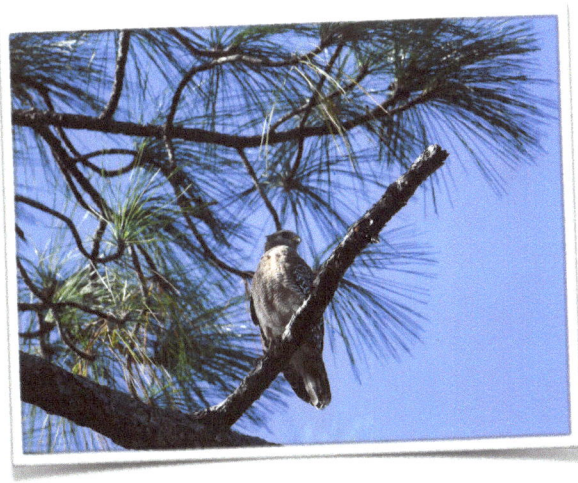
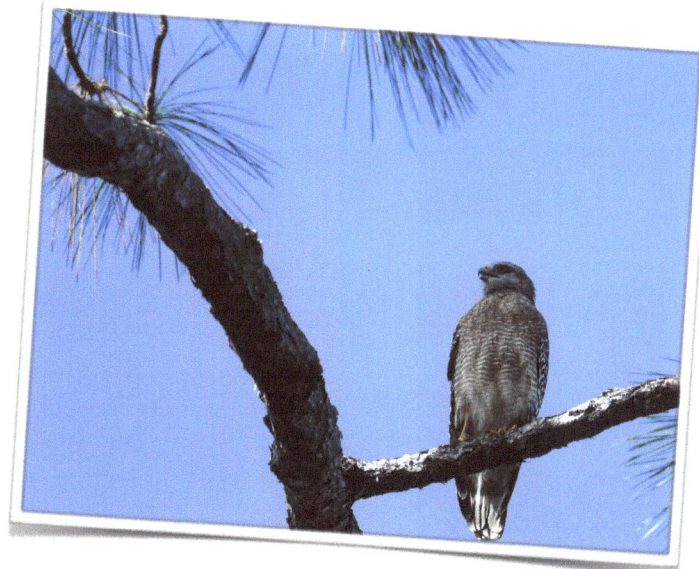

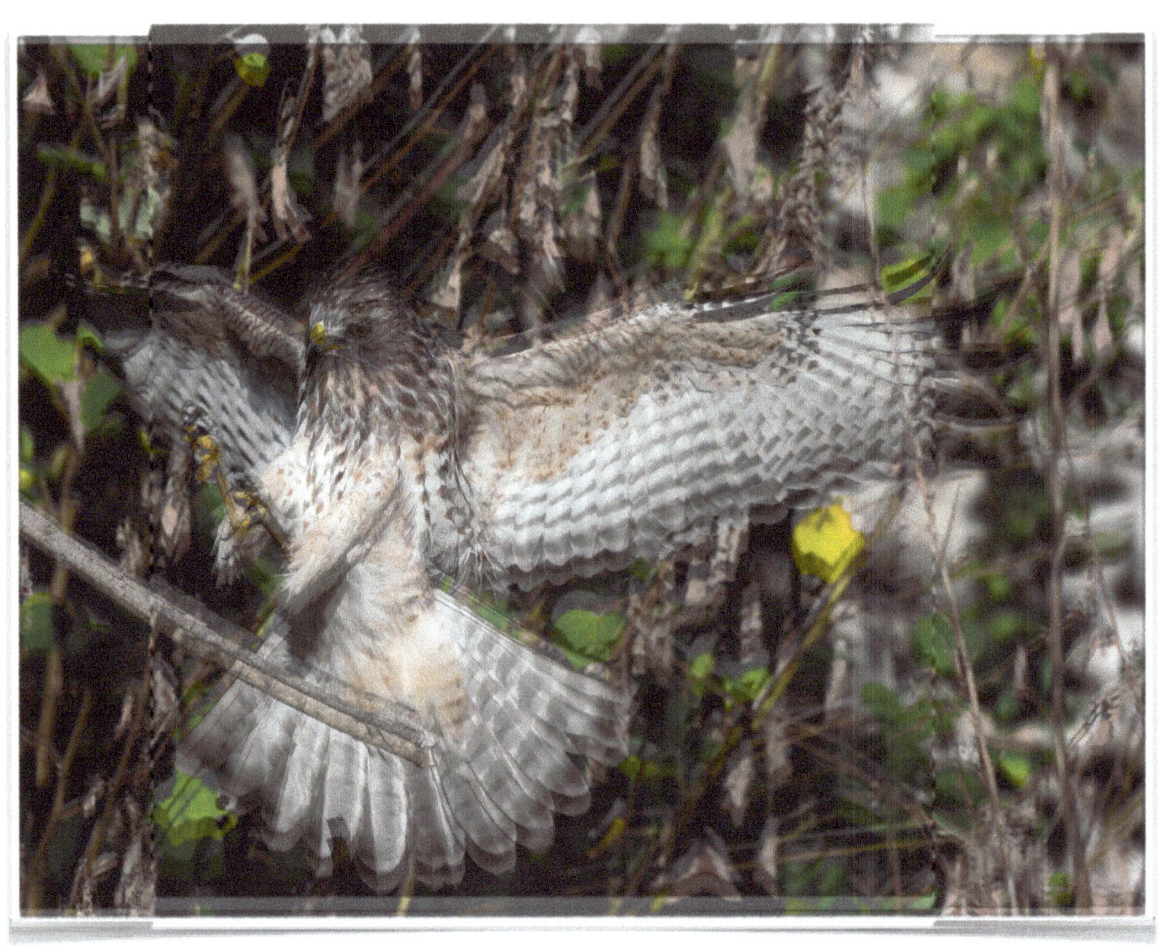
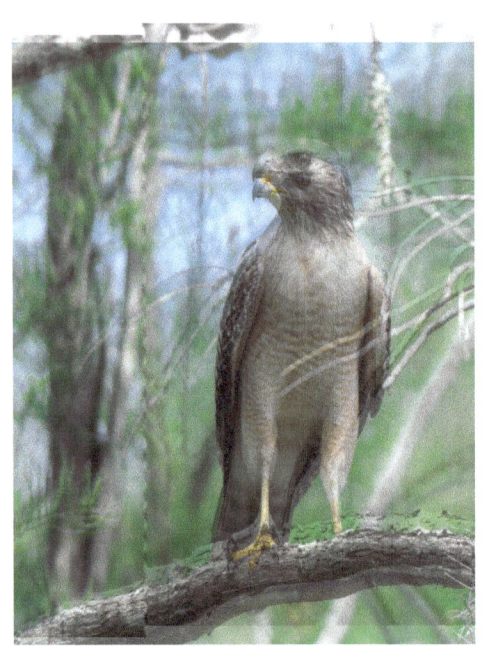
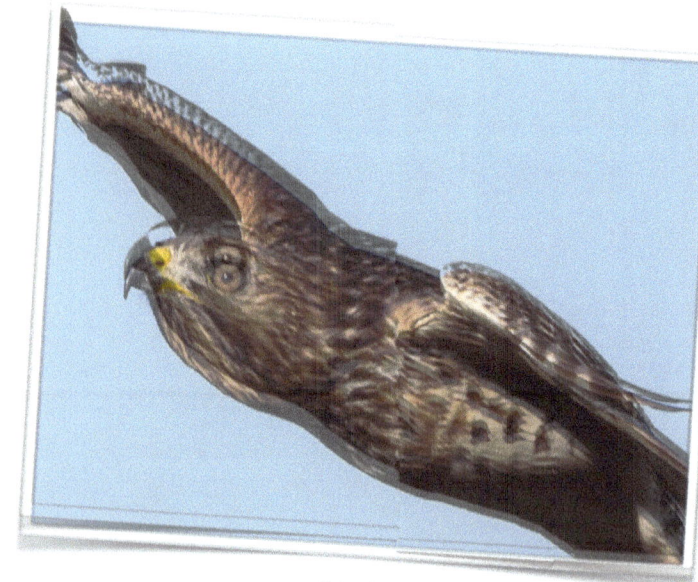

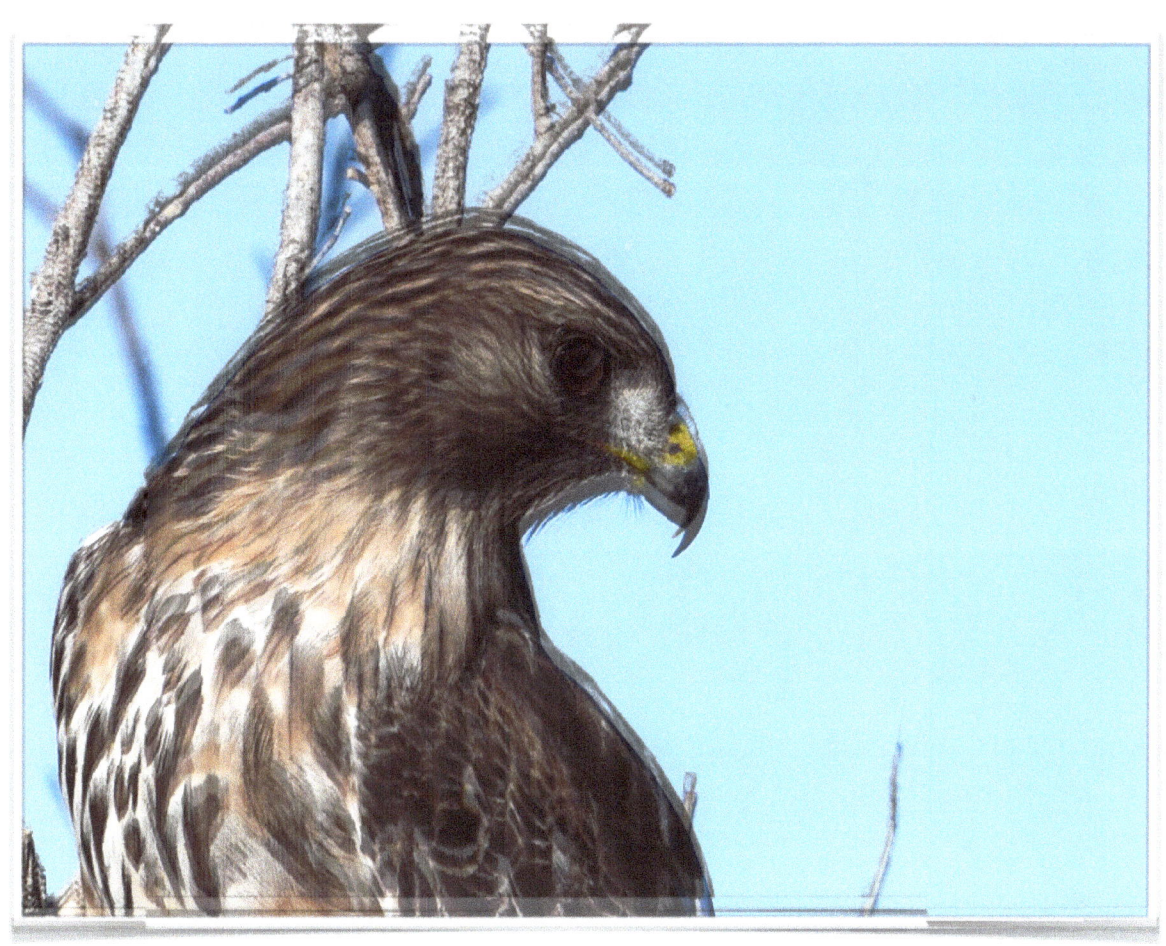
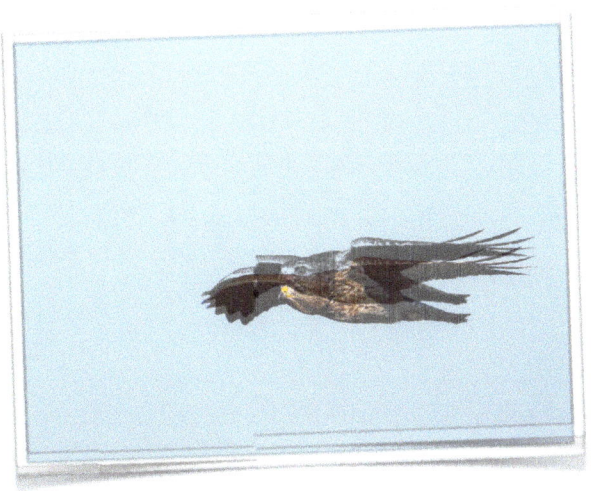
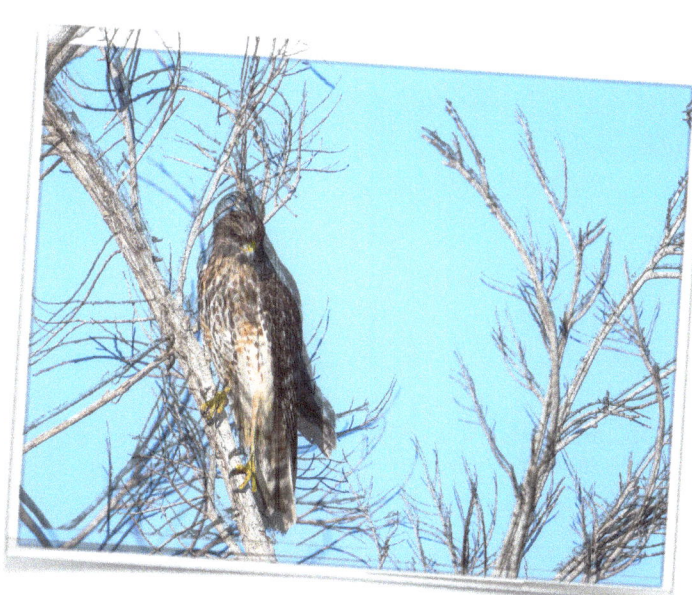

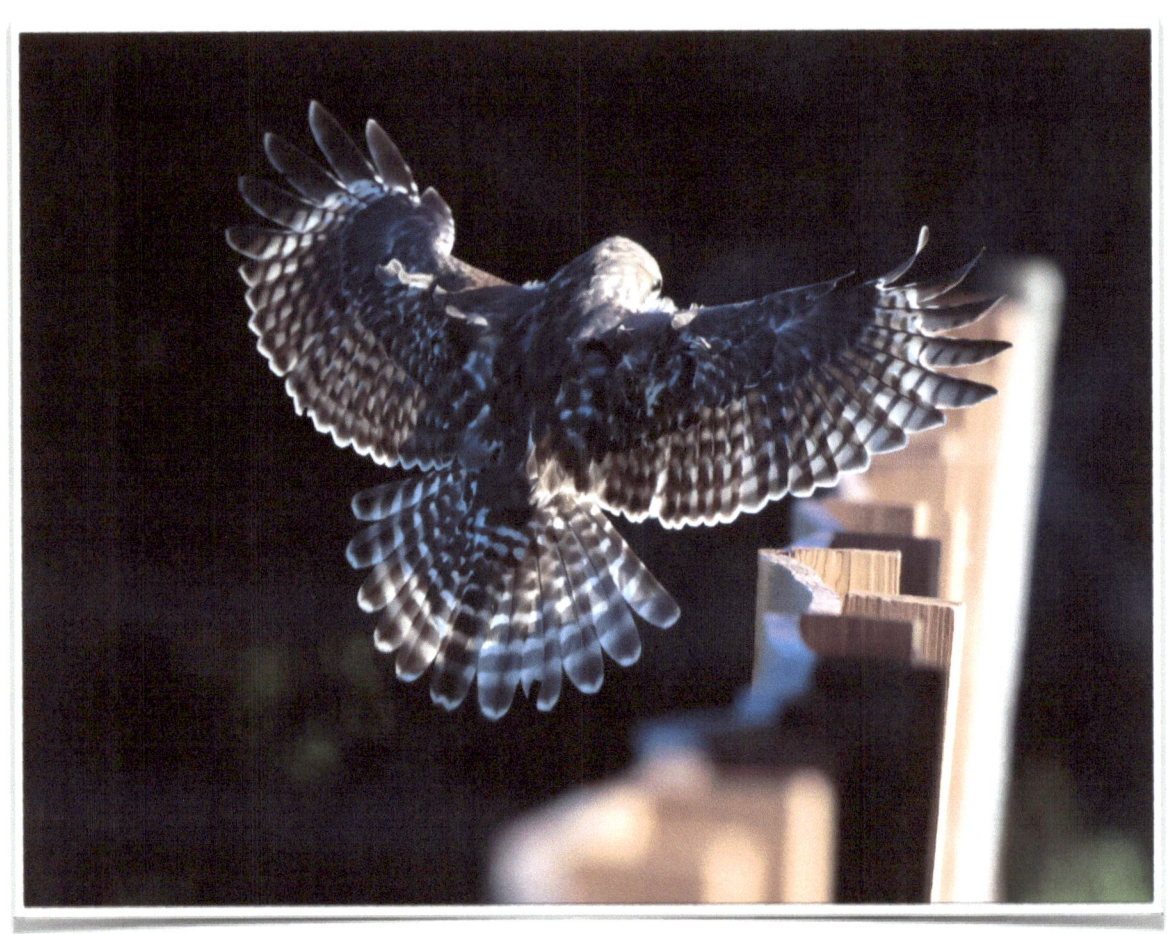
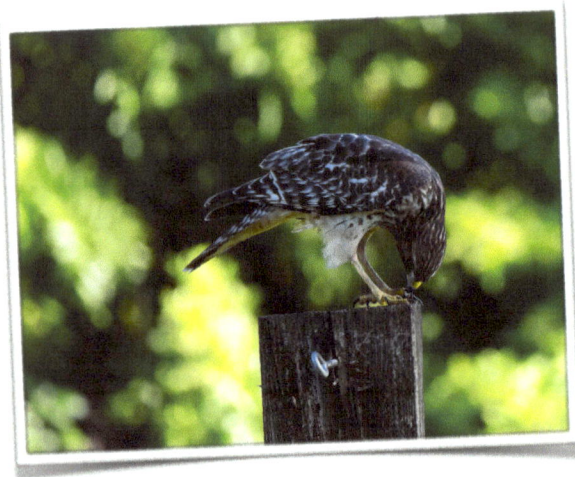
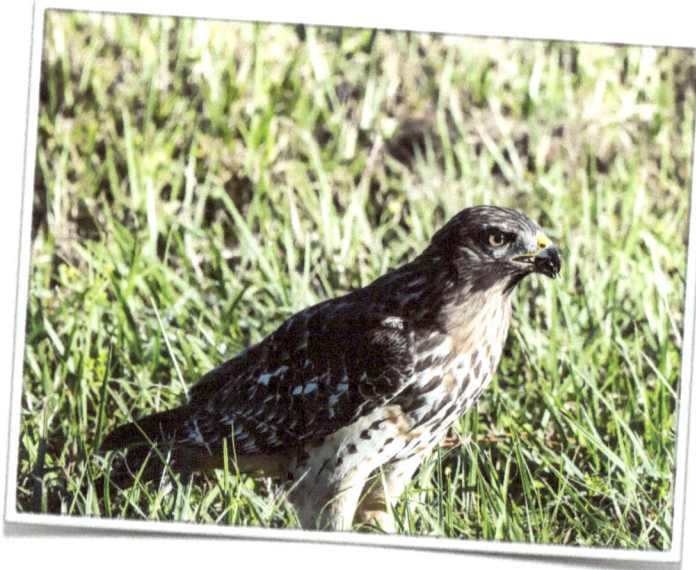

Burrowing Owls

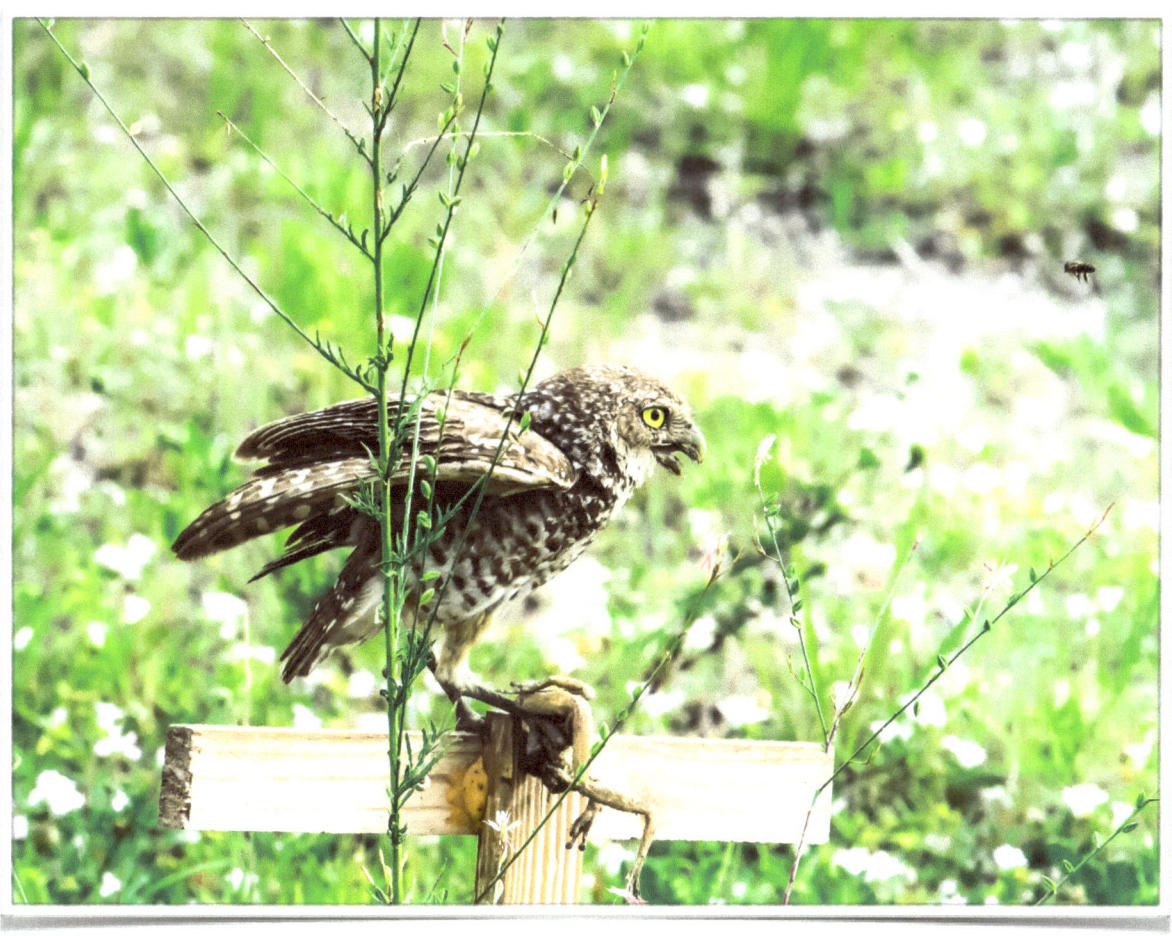

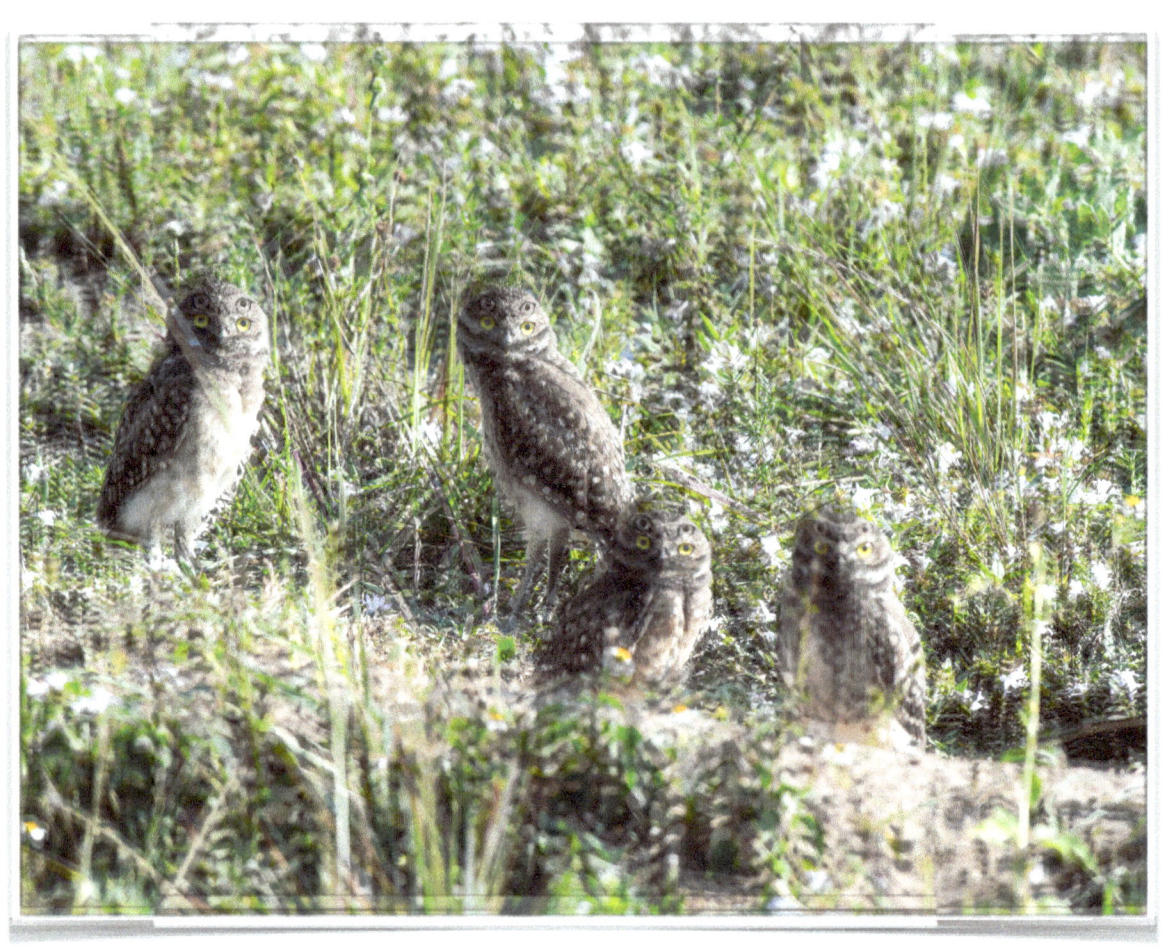
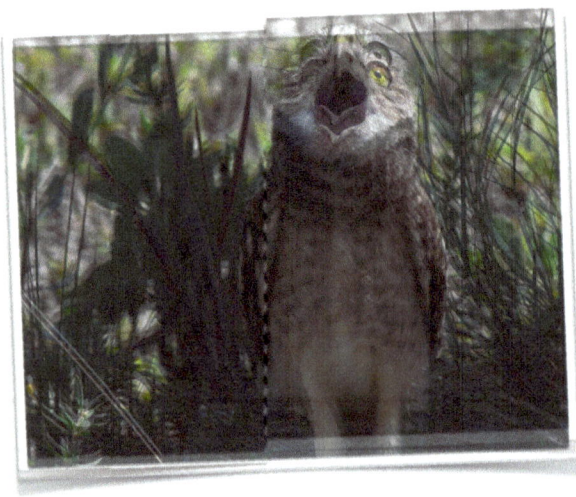
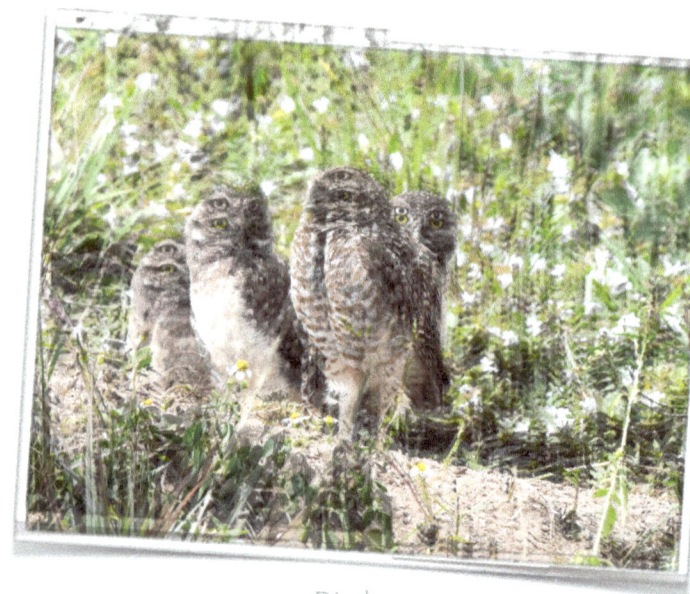

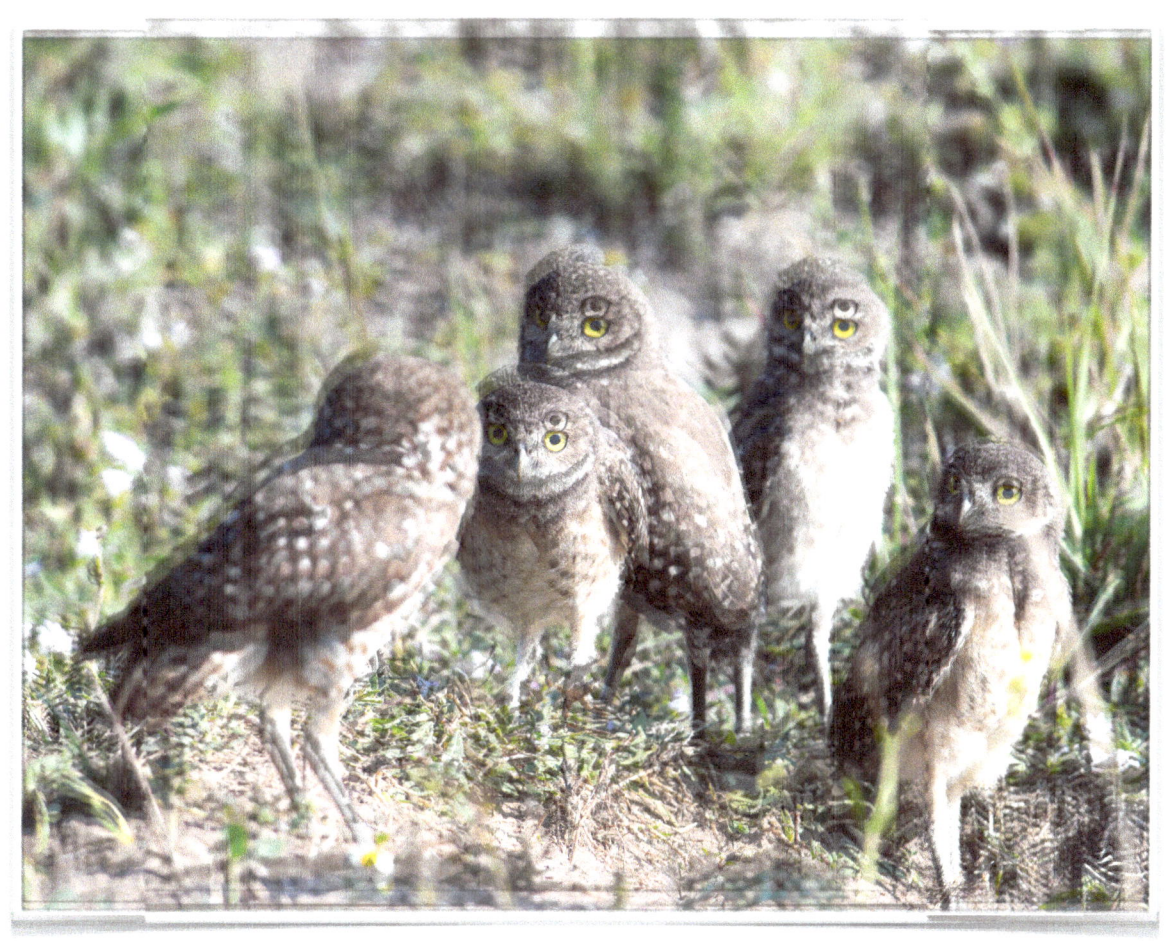
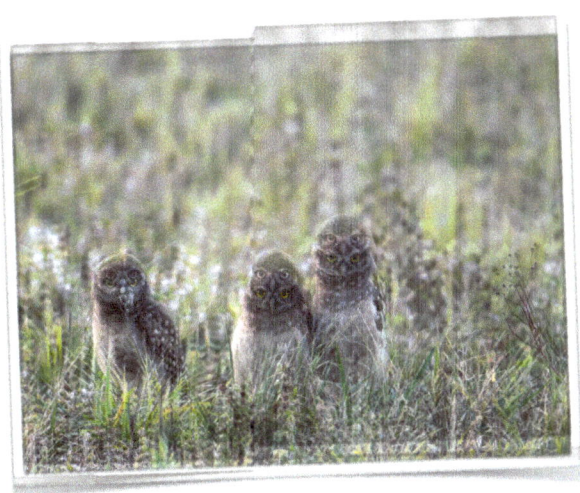
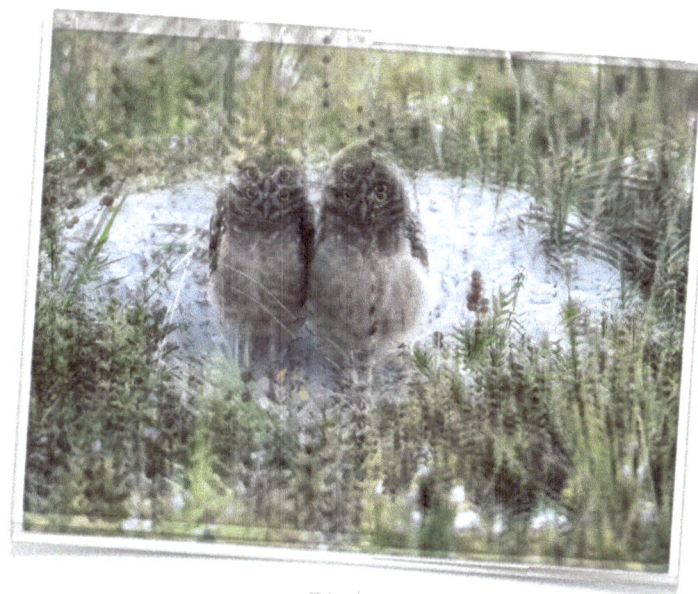

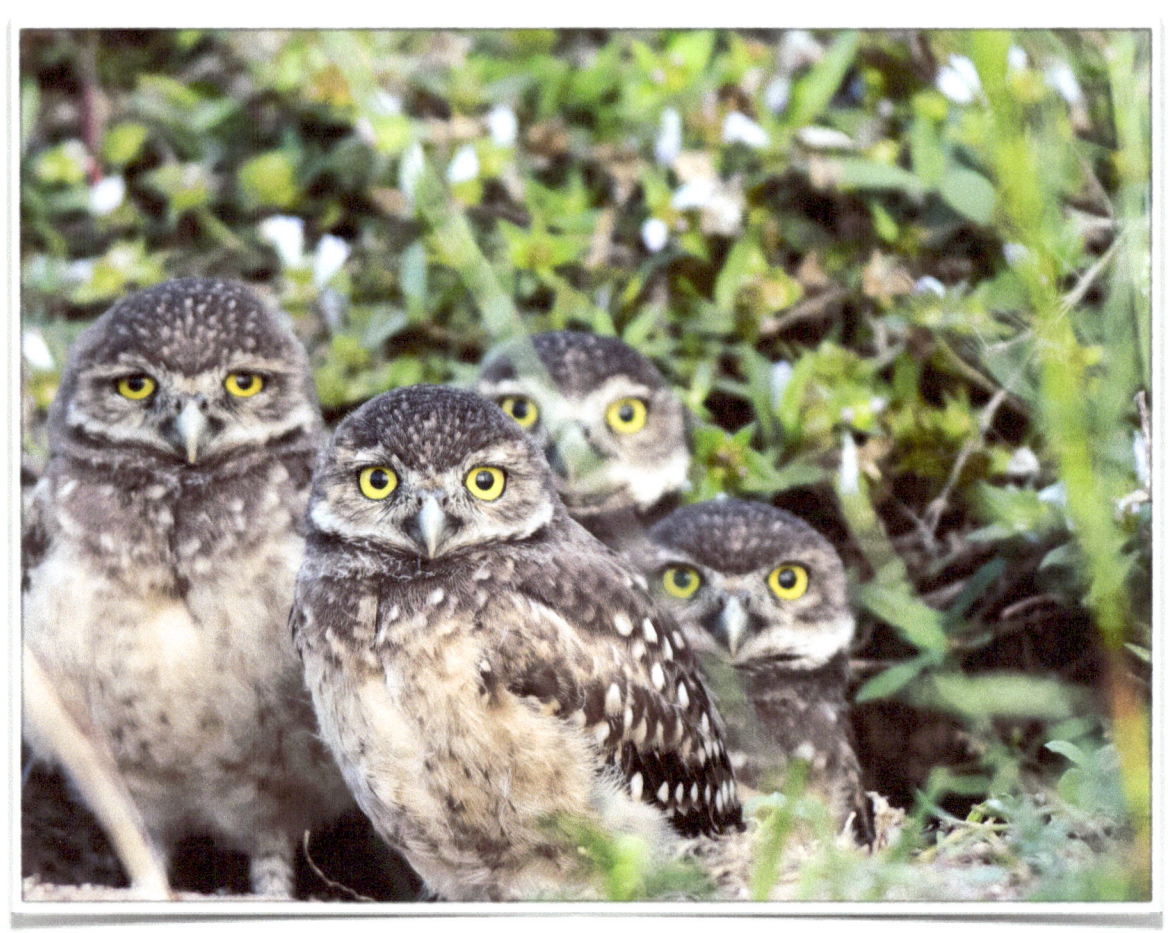
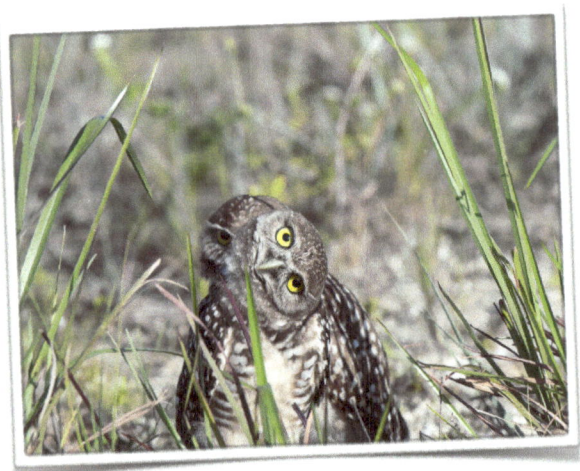
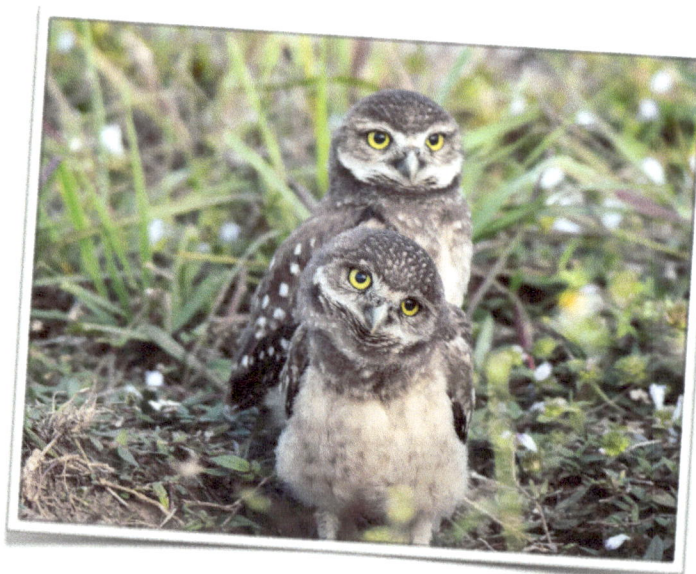

Crested Caracaras

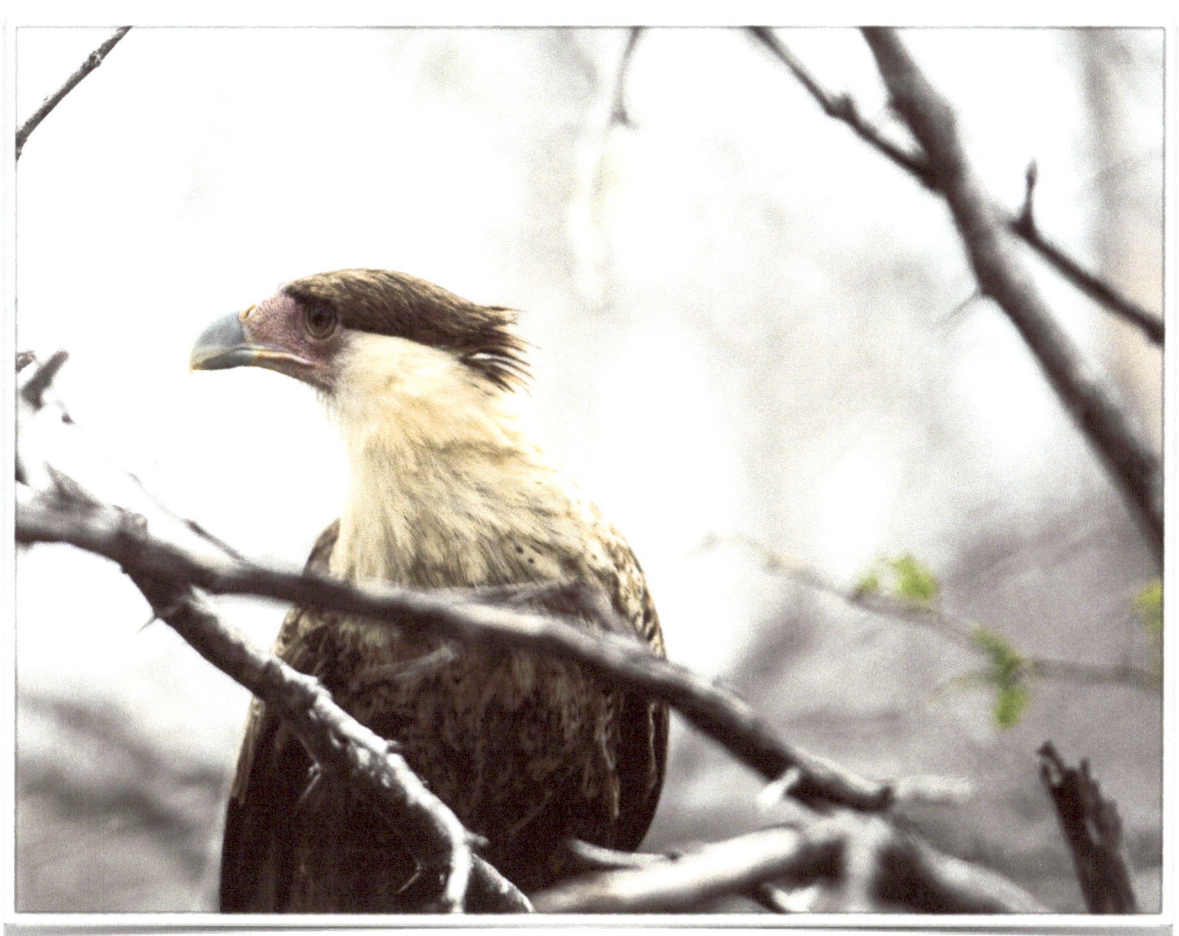

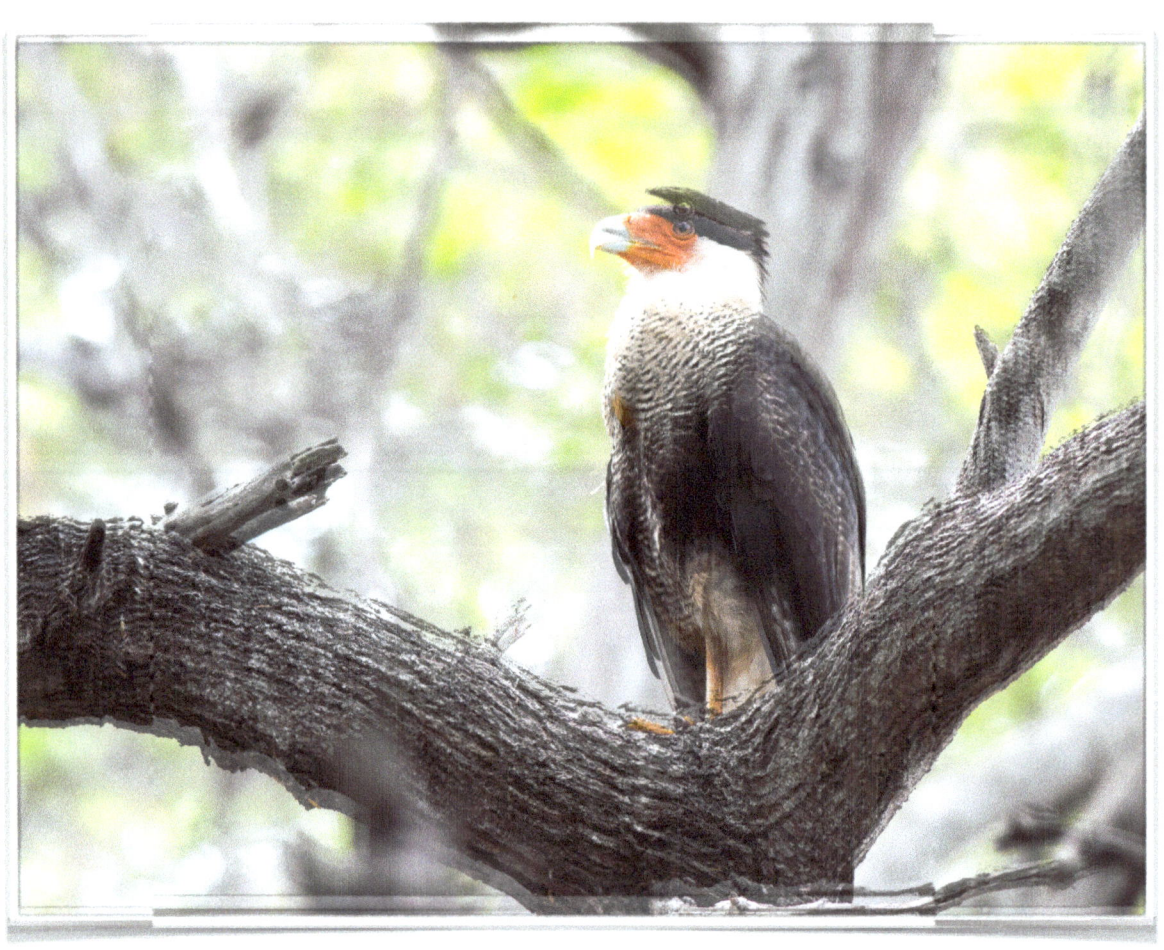
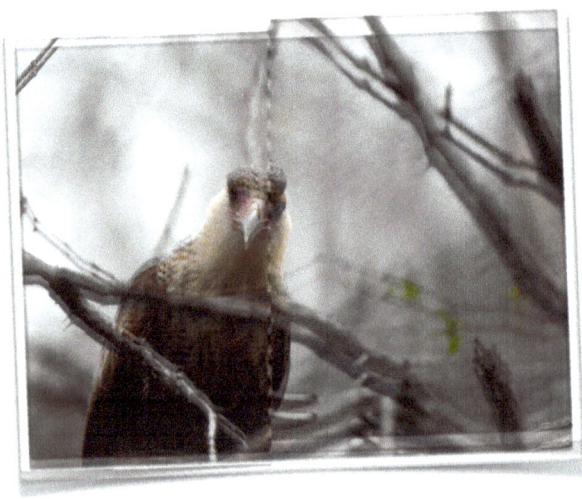
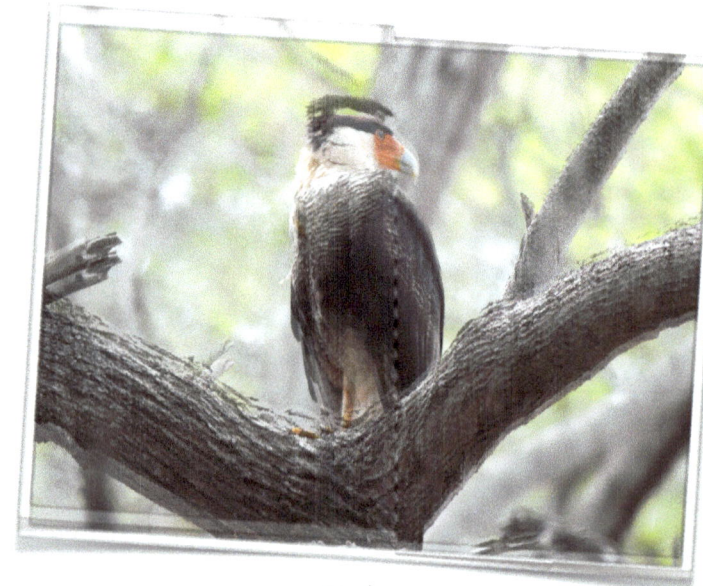

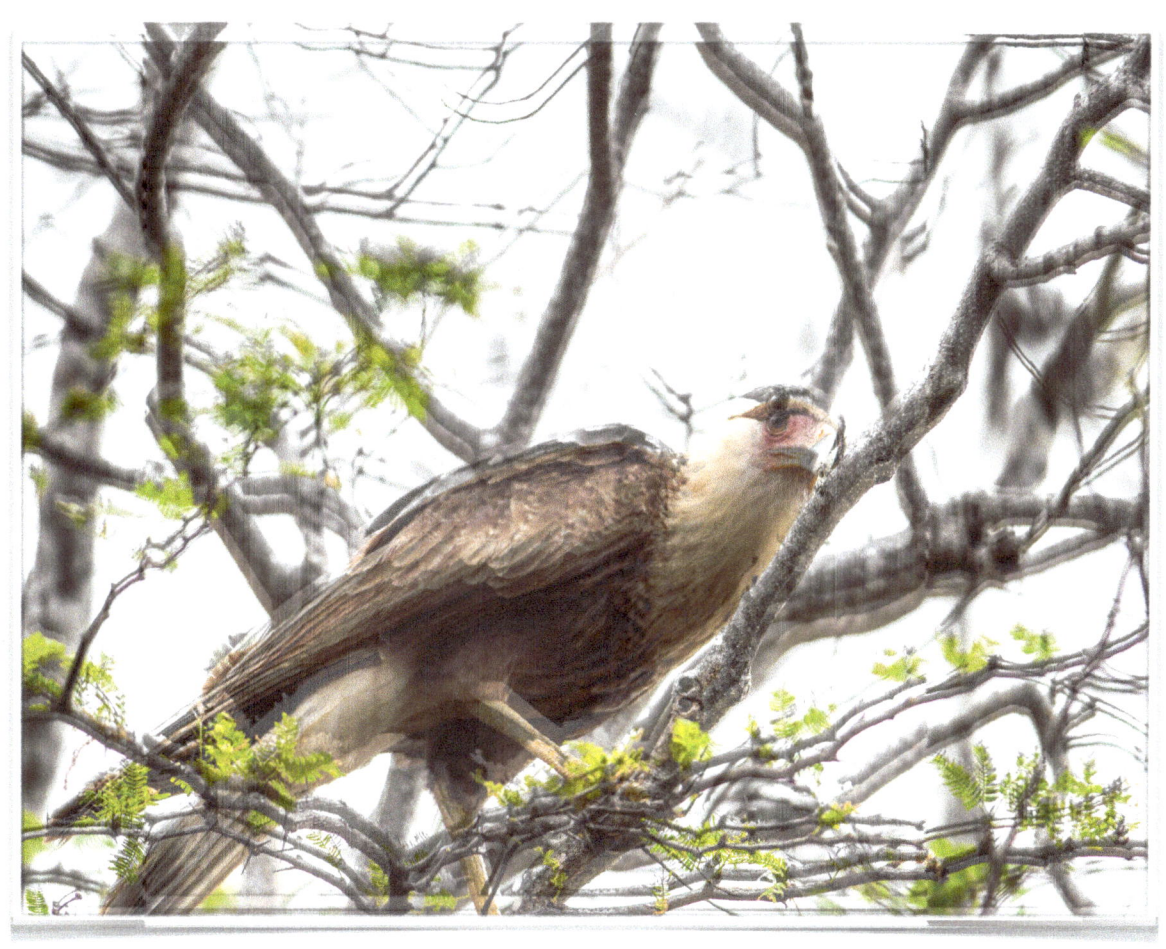
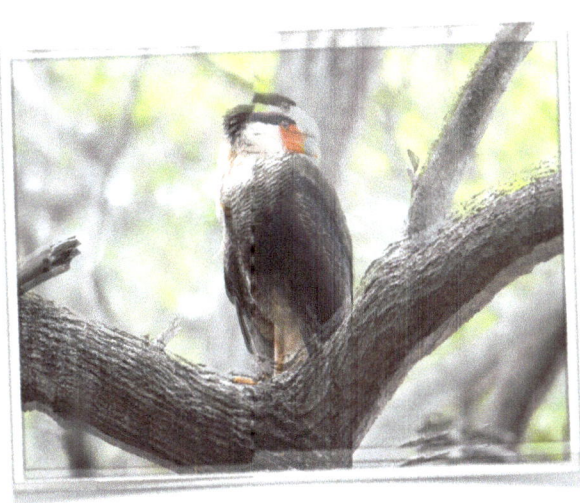
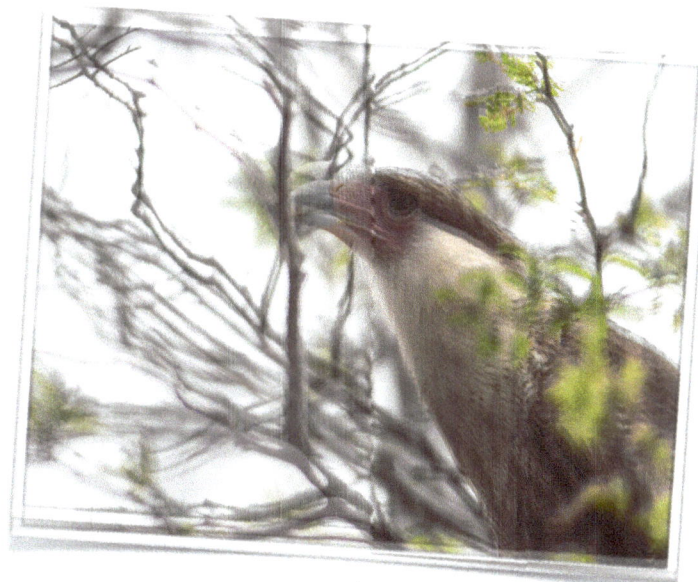

About the Photographer

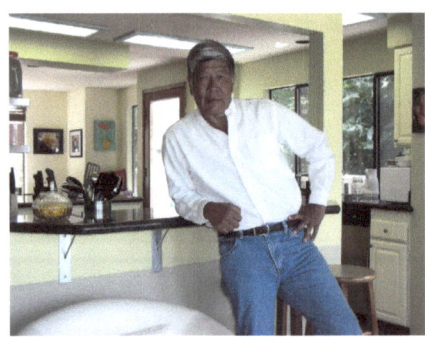

Norman Wei is a nature photographer and environmental consultant who travels the world in search of exotic birds and wildlife. The photographs in this book were taken in Florida and the Caribbean Island of Bonaire.

Prints and enlargements of Norman's photographs can be purchased at www.photosbynormanwei.com. There are photographs of bald eagles, ospreys, pelicans, burrowing owls, hummingbirds, herons, dragonflies, butterflies, hawks, crested caracara, bananaquits, yellow-throated parrots, monk parakeets, painted buntings, bluejays and many other birds and wildlife on the website and more are added weekly.

Norman lives in Cape Coral, Florida with his lovely partner Cathy and several lovebirds. He is also active in scubas diving (underwater macrophotography), standup paddle boarding, kayaking, cycling and flying drones.

He can be reached at photos@normanwei.com.

www.ingramcontent.com/pod-product-compliance
Lightning Source LLC
Chambersburg PA
CBHW051939210526
45473CB00006B/2305